SECOND EDITION

Everybody Move!

A Multimedia Package for Daily Physical Activity

CIRA Ontario

Human Kinetics

Library of Congress Cataloging-in-Publication Data

Everybody move! : a multimedia package for daily physical activity / CIRA Ontario ; John Byl ... [et al.] -- 2nd ed.
    p. cm.
   Previous ed. not in LC.
   Includes bibliographical references.
   ISBN-13: 978-0-7360-8231-0 (soft cover)
   ISBN-10: 0-7360-8231-X (soft cover)
  1. Physical education for children--Curricula. 2. Movement education--Curricula. 3. Exercise for children--Curricula.
I. Byl, John. II. CIRA Ontario.
   GV443.E89 2009
   613.7'042--dc22

                                       2009014463

ISBN-10: 0-7360-8231-X
ISBN-13: 978-0-7360-8231-0

The Web addresses cited in this text were current as of August 13, 2009, unless otherwise noted.

Authors: John Byl, Marie Burland, Mary Dyck, Michelle Hearn, Kirstin Schwass, Milena "Mel" Trojanovic
Acquisitions Editor: Judy Patterson Wright, PhD
Developmental Editor: Bethany J. Bentley
Assistant Editors: Anne Rumery and Elizabeth Evans
Copyeditor: Patricia L. MacDonald
Permission Manager: Dalene Reeder
Graphic Designer: Fred Starbird
Graphic Artist: Patrick Sandberg
Cover Designer: Bob Reuther
Art Manager: Kelly Hendren
Associate Art Manager: Alan L. Wilborn
Illustrator (interior and cover): Stephanie Webb
Printer: United Graphics

Printed in the United States of America   10 9 8 7 6 5 4 3 2 1

The paper in this book is certified under a sustainable forestry program.

Human Kinetics
Web site: www.HumanKinetics.com

United States: Human Kinetics
P.O. Box 5076
Champaign, IL 61825-5076
800-747-4457
e-mail: humank@hkusa.com

Canada: Human Kinetics
475 Devonshire Road Unit 100
Windsor, ON N8Y 2L5
800-465-7301 (in Canada only)
e-mail: info@hkcanada.com

Europe: Human Kinetics
107 Bradford Road
Stanningley
Leeds LS28 6AT, United Kingdom
+44 (0) 113 255 5665
e-mail: hk@hkeurope.com

Australia: Human Kinetics
57A Price Avenue
Lower Mitcham, South Australia 5062
08 8372 0999
e-mail: info@hkaustralia.com

New Zealand: Human Kinetics
Division of Sports Distributors NZ Ltd.
P.O. Box 300 226 Albany
North Shore City
Auckland
0064 9 448 1207
e-mail: info@humankinetics.co.nz

E4783

Contents

Activity Finder   v

How to Use This Book, DVD-ROM, and Music CD   xiv

Acknowledgments   xv

Part I GET READY!

Setting Up a Daily Physical Activity Program

Setting Up a Daily Physical Activity Program • • • • • • • 1

Chapter 1 Why Should Everybody Move? • • • • • •3

Chapter 2 Developing a Daily Physical Activity Program • • • •13

Part II GET MOVING!

Fun Fitness Activities

Fun Fitness Activities • • • • • • • • 29

Chapter 3 Fun Fitness Activities in the Classroom • • • • • • • • • 31

Chapter 4 Activities for Spaces In and Around the Building • • • • • 69

Chapter 5 Outdoor Activities • • • • • • 85

Chapter 6 Themed Activities • • • • • • 95

Part III GET MOVING TO MUSIC!

Funky Moves and Group Routines • • 119

Chapter 7 Move It to the Beat—
Actions for Music • • • • • • • • • • • 121

Chapter 8 Ready-to-Use Routines—
Dances and Routines
on the DVD-ROM • • • • • • • • • • 133

Chapter 9 Routines for Accessible Music • • • • 167

Part IV
GET EVERYBODY ON BOARD!

Gaining Program Support
and Assessing Your Program • • • • 205

Chapter 10 Supporting Your DPA program • • • 207

Chapter 11 Assessing Your DPA program • • • • 213

Appendix A   Glossary of Fitness Activities   221

Appendix B   Sample Newsletter   223

Appendix C   Success Stories   227

References and Resources   231

About CIRA Ontario   234

About the Contributors   235

DVD-ROM User Instructions   239

CD and DVD Contents   240

Activity Finder

Activity	Page number	Space needed	Equipment	Accompanying track on CD	Accompanying activity cards on DVD-ROM
30-Second Exercises	38	Classroom	Index cards and pens or pencils	Elementary or high school circuit	
Aerobics	146	Classroom or large open space	CD player and music CD	9. Aerobics	Cue sheet
Agadoo	188	Classroom, though a larger open space is preferred	CD player and music CD		
Amazing Race	56	Classroom	4 pylons, 4 skipping ropes, 20 tennis balls, 1 small pail, 4 beanbags, 4 pool noodles	Elementary or high school circuit	Station cards
Animal Walks	37	Classroom	None required		
Around the World Fitness Relay	116	Playground or gymnasium	Scorecards and pencils, hoops or rope for airplanes		Air Traffic Controller Card Scorecards
Athletic Moves	40	Classroom	None required	Elementary or high school circuit	
Balloon Keep-Up	61	Classroom	1 balloon per group		
Beanbag Tag	92	Field or large open room	1 beanbag per player, a pool noodle for each "it," 4 pylons to mark playing area		
Bicycle Races	34	Classroom	2 desks or tables placed closely together	21. Stadium Rock	
Boxercise	149	Classroom, though a larger open space is preferred	CD player and music CD	10. Boxercise	Cue sheet

Activity	Page number	Space needed	Equipment	Accompanying track on CD	Accompanying activity cards on DVD-ROM
Bring It All Back	174	Classroom, though a larger open space is preferred	CD player and music CD		
Bye-Bye	51	Classroom	Desks or hula hoops		
Capture the Flag	89	Large field	Flags, 2 sets of different-colored pinnies, 8 pylons		
Celebrate Winter	103	Classroom	Recycled paper		Winter circuit
Chair Aerobics	65	Classroom	1 chair for each person	Any of the get-moving songs or the cool-down songs	
Chicken Dance	193	Classroom, though a larger open space is preferred	CD player and music CD		Cue sheet
Chuck the Chicken	83	Field or large open room	1 rubber chicken		
Classroom Foosball	62	Classroom	Masking tape, 1 chair per player, Gator Skin ball or Nerf soccer ball, 4 pylons		
Classroom Triathlon	60	Classroom	Chairs to sit on (optional)		
Climbers and Sliders	58	Classroom	1 Climbers and Sliders board per group, 1 die and 1 marker per board; have players imagine when equipment is suggested (or provide it: skipping ropes, basketballs, hula hoops, and so on)		100 Activities Chart Playing board

Activity	Page number	Space needed	Equipment	Accompanying track on CD	Accompanying activity cards on DVD-ROM
Cotton-Eyed Joe	184	Classroom, though a larger open space is preferred	CD player and music CD		Cue sheet
Cupid's Arrow	109	Classrooms	Fitness card arrow		
Dance to the Music	185	Classroom, though a larger open space is preferred	CD player and music CD		Cue sheet
Disc Golf Race	87	Large outdoor area	1 disc per pair of players; recording sheet (optional)		Recording sheet
Doghouse	88	Field or large open room	Popsicle sticks (equal numbers of 4 colors), 4 pylons		
Dream Machine	144	Classroom, though a larger open space is preferred	CD player and music CD	7. Dream Machine	Cue sheet
Eddie the Razor	135	Classroom, though a larger open space is preferred	CD player and music CD	2. Eddie the Razor	Cue sheet
Ethno Tension (African Routine)	161	Classroom, though a larger open space is preferred	CD player and music CD	8. Ethno Tension	Cue sheet
Fall Frenzy	102	Classroom, though a larger open space is preferred	Construction paper, a pair of gloves, balloons	Elementary or high school circuit	
Fitness Circuit	80	Room of sufficient size for stations for small groups	Station instruction cards printed from DVD-ROM	Elementary or high school circuit	1 of 3 circuits
Fitness Roll	39	Classroom	Scrap paper, 15-20 pairs of dice		

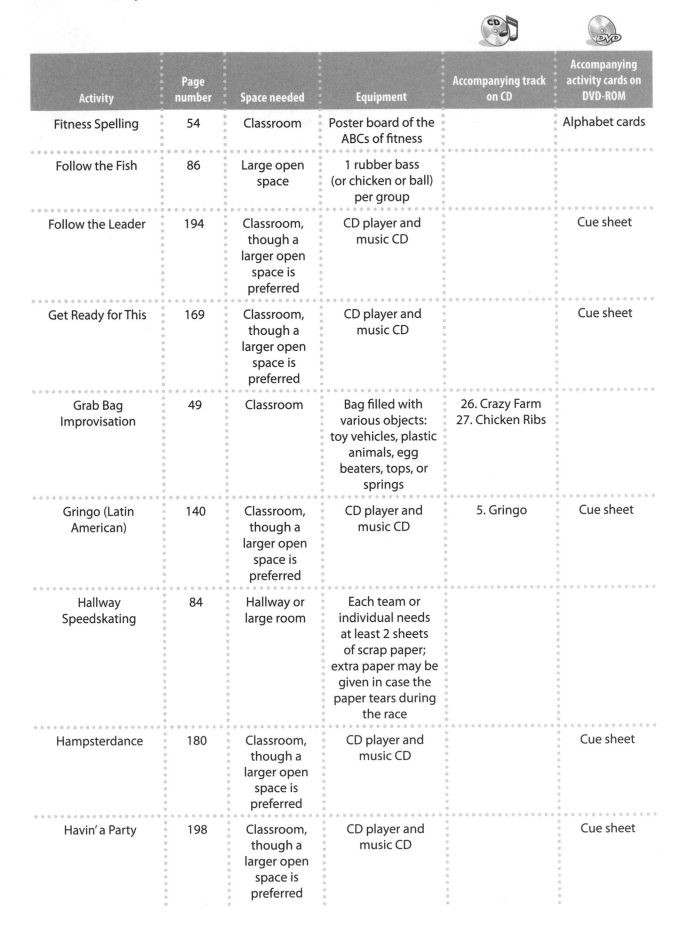

Activity	Page number	Space needed	Equipment	Accompanying track on CD	Accompanying activity cards on DVD-ROM
Fitness Spelling	54	Classroom	Poster board of the ABCs of fitness		Alphabet cards
Follow the Fish	86	Large open space	1 rubber bass (or chicken or ball) per group		
Follow the Leader	194	Classroom, though a larger open space is preferred	CD player and music CD		Cue sheet
Get Ready for This	169	Classroom, though a larger open space is preferred	CD player and music CD		Cue sheet
Grab Bag Improvisation	49	Classroom	Bag filled with various objects: toy vehicles, plastic animals, egg beaters, tops, or springs	26. Crazy Farm 27. Chicken Ribs	
Gringo (Latin American)	140	Classroom, though a larger open space is preferred	CD player and music CD	5. Gringo	Cue sheet
Hallway Speedskating	84	Hallway or large room	Each team or individual needs at least 2 sheets of scrap paper; extra paper may be given in case the paper tears during the race		
Hampsterdance	180	Classroom, though a larger open space is preferred	CD player and music CD		Cue sheet
Havin' a Party	198	Classroom, though a larger open space is preferred	CD player and music CD		Cue sheet

Activity	Page number	Space needed	Equipment	Accompanying track on CD	Accompanying activity cards on DVD-ROM
Healthy Simon Says	44	Classroom	A list of health and active living questions		
Heart Fitness Circuit	112	Classroom or large room	Red paper, scissors, pencils		Heart Fitness Circuit cards
Heart Smart	118	Classroom or large room	Pictures of food groups with suggested activities	Any of the get-moving songs or either of the circuits	Food Group Exercises
Hey Baby	172	Classroom, though a larger open space is preferred	CD player and music CD		Cue sheet
I Will Survive	200	Classroom, though a larger open space is preferred	CD player and music CD		Cue sheet
Jump the Answer	48	Classroom			
Jumping Beans	35	Classroom	A large chart listing the bean names and corresponding activities (optional)	Any of the get-moving songs	
Keep It Up Team Challenge	72	Open space	3 pylons per team, 1 balloon per team, 20 scrap-paper balls		
Kokomo	186	Classroom, though a larger open space is preferred	CD player and music CD		Cue sheet
Latin Mix	152	Classroom, though a larger open space is preferred	CD player and music CD	11. Mambo Jumbo 12. Cumbia Urbana 13. Reggaeton Tripiac 14. Lucky 6	Cue sheet

Activity	Page number	Space needed	Equipment	Accompanying track on CD	Accompanying activity cards on DVD-ROM
Latinique	142	Classroom, though a larger open space is preferred	CD player and music CD	6. Latinique	Cue sheet
Line 'em Up	73	Open space the size of a volleyball court	1 pool noodle per bulldog, large empty room with lots of lines on the floor		
Line Jump	33	Classroom	Masking tape or string to make lines	4. Marching Circus 21. Stadium Rock	
Lollipop	190	Classroom, though a larger open space is preferred	CD player and music CD		Cue sheet
Magnetic Force Field	46	Classroom	None required		
Marching Circus	138	Classroom, though a larger open space is preferred	CD player and music CD	4. Marching Circus	Cue sheet
Math Match	52	Classroom	Question and answer cards		Math cards Verb cards Locomotor cards
Mission Possible	70	Any room	Mission cards for every 3 players, 6 skipping ropes (players can pretend if you do not have any), 6 hula hoops (players can pretend if you do not have any)	20. Mission Improbable	Mission list
Motion Motion	136	Classroom, though a larger open space is preferred	CD player and music CD	3. Motion Motion	Cue sheet

Activity	Page number	Space needed	Equipment	Accompanying track on CD	Accompanying activity cards on DVD-ROM
Move This	197	Classroom, though a larger open space is preferred	CD player and music CD		Cue sheet
Pass the Bass	32	Classroom	1 rubber bass (or rubber chicken or other rubber animal or a beanbag or tennis ball) per group	Any of the get-moving songs or the cool-down songs	
Pinball	63	Classroom	1 chair per player, 1 Gator Skin ball or Nerf soccer ball		
Popcorn	182	Classroom, though a larger open space is preferred	CD player and music CD		Cue sheet
Practice Tag	47	Classroom	None required, although a pool noodle for each "it" is safer and more fun		
Reach	177	Classroom, though a larger open space is preferred	CD player and music CD		Cue sheet
Robin's Nest	78	Large open space	1 hula hoop per group, 8-12 small objects (balls, stuffed animals, clothespins)		
Rock Around the Clock	196	Classroom, though a larger open space is preferred	CD player and music CD		Cue sheet
Scarf Patterns	50	Classroom	1 scarf per player, index cards and pens or pencils, and chalk and board	37. Shammusa	

Activity	Page number	Space needed	Equipment	Accompanying track on CD	Accompanying activity cards on DVD-ROM
Smile	162	Classroom, though a larger open space is preferred	CD player and music CD	1. Smile	Cue sheet
Smile Yoga	163	Classroom, though a larger open space is preferred	CD player and music CD	1. Smile	Cue sheet
Speed Simon Says	42	Classroom	None required		
Speed-Walk Shuffle	41	Classroom	30-40 marbles (or trashballs, beanbags, math manipulatives, popsicle sticks . . .)	Lively music like: 16. Rock Shot 17. Rock and Roll	
Spelling Relay	64	Classroom	200 popsicle sticks (buy from most dollar stores)		
Spring Energy/ Chinese New Year/ Easter Egg Hunt	113	Classroom or gymnasium	Plastic eggs or Chinese New Year envelopes, small pieces of paper with activities written on them	6. Latinique	List of activities
Spring: One-Minute Survivor Fitness	110	Classroom or gymnasium	Beanbags, pylons, skipping ropes	Lively music like: 21. Stadium Rock	Survivor Fitness sheets
Stair Step-Ups	74	Stairs	None required	16. Rock Shot	
Summer Olympics	100	Field or large open room	Station sheets printed from DVD-ROM, balls or beanbags, baton, beach ball, scooter boards	21. Stadium Rock	12 station sheets
Train Tag	93	Field or large open room	4 pylons to mark playing area		
Trashball Tricks	36	Classroom	1 piece of scrap paper per player, or several sheets of newspaper and masking tape, or Hacky Sacks, tennis balls, or any other small balls		

Activity	Page number	Space needed	Equipment	Accompanying track on CD	Accompanying activity cards on DVD-ROM
Triangle Tag	77	Field or large open room	1 pinny per group		
Uncrate the Sun	106	Gymnasium	2 hula hoops, 1 beach ball, bucket of sand, 1 spoon, broom, golf putter, golf ball, golf target, 3 scooters, 1 Wiffle ball, some string, dress-up clothes, 4 flying discs	36. Jammin' Mon	Uncrate the Sun station cards
Up	192	Classroom, though a larger open space is preferred	CD player and music CD		Cue sheet
Vita Parcours	90	Outdoor area or inside a building	Laminated cards		Station cards
Walk Across Your Country	96	Walking or jogging route marked for distance	Map of country		
We Like to Party	202	Classroom, though a larger open space is preferred	CD player and music CD		Cue sheet
Who's Coming?	53	Classroom	None required	6. Latinique 21. Stadium Rock	
Winner's Olympics	98	Classroom or large room	Station cards printed from DVD-ROM	21. Stadium Rock	20 station cards

How to Use This Book, DVD-ROM, and Music CD

Let's move! Active lifestyles help all people, especially school children, to optimize their health and enjoyment of life. On the flip side, we have all read and heard the statistics on growing obesity and the amount of sedentary time people spend in front of television and computer screens. Too much sitting around numbs the mind, making it all the more important to emphasize that everybody move!

This resource was initiated by teachers who are committed to keeping students active and are concerned about the health of children in their schools. These teachers experienced success with various daily fitness breaks for their students and also with seniors and wanted to share their ideas with you. This resource has three components: this book, a music CD, and a DVD-ROM that shows demonstrations of the choreography for some of the activity breaks, shows demonstrations of funky moves described in the book, and also includes 235 reproducible forms and activity cards that you can easily print out for use in your own classrooms. Regardless of your expertise, this entire turnkey resource will help you begin a program of daily physical activity breaks.

Part I of the book provides the rationale for the project and instructions on using *Everybody Move!* at your school or facility. Part II provides information on engaging in fun fitness activities using various themes in a room, in locations throughout a larger building, or outdoors. Routines for music and some generic and funky moves to add delight to your program are found in part III. Part IV presents some samples and ideas to get your program moving and suggestions for dealing with assessment.

The *Everybody Move!* music CD included with this resource helps you get started with some great tunes. Some of the tunes are for dance routines, others can be used when doing a circuit in 30-second time blocks, and all can inspire movement when used as background music while doing any of the physical activities described in this resource.

The *Everybody Move!* DVD-ROM allows you to visualize the routine instructions; remember that activity rather than perfect form is the key. Once you start, you can develop other motivational activities and gather other music that will energize your participants. The DVD-ROM also includes 235 activity cards that you can easily print out to use with activities in the book. A thumbnail of each card is shown with the activity in the book for your reference. Note that in instances where there are a large number of pages for a set of cards, we have shown just a sampling of what is included on the DVD-ROM.

Whether you are leading younger or older children, this resource helps you make a positive difference in their lives. Your efforts, through the help of this resource, will make great strides in helping everybody move!

Acknowledgments

This resource has been developed by CIRA Ontario to advance its mission of promoting fun, active participation for all through intramurals and recreation. It is important to briefly discuss the resource's history and to thank the many people who made this project possible.

Marie Burland, from Robert Little Public School, provided the original inspiration for this project. She was doing aerobic dances with her young students and a group of local senior citizens. Marie shared these dance initiatives on the CIRA Ontario listserv. Many people e-mailed her asking for more information. She thought the best way to help everyone was to write a resource on moving to music. She contacted me, and I was persuaded to begin preparing this resource immediately. Once the project was on its way, Marie provided incredible enthusiasm, energy, a positive attitude, dedication, and her dancing experience with students and seniors.

We could not have done this resource on our own. Three other teachers were also actively encouraging movement to music and promoting daily physical activity: Michelle Hearn, Kirstin Schwass, and Mel Trojanovic. Michelle, from Highland Public School, our dance and fitness expert, contributed significantly to the dance choreography for the DVD-ROM and the book. She always brought a positive attitude and had a knack for creating routines. Watching Michelle get up and demonstrate some funky moves or dance routines made everyone want to get up and join in the fun. Kirstin, from Morton Way Public School, is known for her energetic work on active assemblies. She brought enthusiasm, energy, and expertise to this project and did amazing work on the dance section. She provided a key role in double-checking all the music on the CDs and the dances and funky moves on the DVD-ROM, ensuring consistency in the dance formats (she was the chief editor of the funky moves). Kirstin models by leading an active lifestyle on a daily basis and puts her own children first. Mel, from C.H. Norton Public School, always encouraged us in the project and made the resource engaging for senior elementary students. Mel brought high energy, great humor, bright sunshine, endless resources, awesome ideas, and fun, fun, fun. Some people may wonder how to motivate intermediate students or boys specifically to participate in dance routines. Mel managed to do both and was a voice for what's cool for kids. Under Mel's direction, "Dream Machine" was choreographed by her class of eighth-grade boys.

Two other people also joined our creative writing and dancing team: Myra Stephen and Mary Dyck. Myra, from Valley Park Middle School, took the lead and did amazing work with the CBC in producing the CD and also worked tirelessly on the production side for the DVD-ROM. She brought a lot of experience to the table and paid meticulous attention to detail. Her feedback was always correct, and she encouraged us with lots of laughs and efficient, careful work. She always wanted to make sure the book would come alive for teachers, recreation leaders, and participants. Mary Dyck, my colleague from Redeemer University College, now at the University of Lethbridge, took the lead on the games chapter; reedited chapters 1, 2, 10, and 11; and also looked sharply at the specific details of the book to make sure it worked effectively for everyone. She encouraged inclusiveness and reminded us that the resource must meet the needs of many different people. Mary applied a logical and hardworking approach. She was thorough in her editing reviews and a voice for those who love being active but shy away from that D word (dance!).

The most amazing aspect of this publication is that all the work was completed by these folks on a volunteer basis. They each saw the vision of this project and wanted to make a difference in the lives of people. The hours and energy spent developing this resource and refining it were substantial. We thank each one of you for your awesome contributions!

Members of the CIRA Ontario executive have a passion for children: They saw the value of the proposed project in June of 2004. They agreed to invest money in the project as a means of encouraging CIRA Ontario's mission. The Ontario Ministry of Tourism and Recreation assisted us with substantial funds to develop a great, original product and train and support others in the goal of helping people, especially children, live active and full lives.

Jacqueline Donkersloot did our initial layout in the summer of 2004. We benefitted immensely from her efficient and careful work in preparing an initial draft on which to build. We refined and improved the content of the book in the fall of 2004. Hannah Braam was then hired to creatively lay out and precisely edit the book, and she did a marvelous job pulling together all of our e-mails and phone calls into a final product. The project was one of occasional meetings and mountains of e-mail! The writers communicated almost entirely by e-mail, and Hannah is to be congratulated for sorting through and determining the changes that were needed. Judith Farris did some final edits to ensure we had written everything correctly. When Human Kinetics agreed to publish this second edition, Bethany Bentley ably took on the role of editing and reformatting this resource into a product that was even more effective.

The Ontario Physical and Health Education Association (Ophea) has long been an advocate for active, healthy children. We used and adapted some of their great ideas. We thank them for creating these ideas and generously granting us permission to share them with you. In particular, we want to thank Steve Soroko for his helpful critique and suggestions near the end of our writing.

Barbara Brown from the CBC gave us a huge start by guiding us in finding motivating music for the CD. She also assisted us in obtaining copyright permissions and in putting many different pieces of music onto one CD. We want to thank Dave Bayley and Sean French for providing us with original music: "Smile" and "Motion Motion."

This resource is meant for people of all ages. We want to thank the children who inspire each of us. We also want to thank the children who worked hard at refining their routines and allowed us to record them for this learning resource. We want to thank some individual children, such as Mel's students Kira Barey and Nadia Barey, who assisted with some of the game ideas for the book. Thanks to Sheela Bharath, acting vice principal of Morton Way Public School, for sharing her African dance experience and helping to choreograph Ethno Tension.

We also want to thank the folks around us who supported us in this venture. Kelly Hare and Michelle Harkness in the CIRA Ontario office were personally supportive of the project and were quick to provide administrative assistance and advice whenever that was needed. We were also supported by family members and friends who saw less of us when we were writing and leading Everybody Move! workshops. Your encouragement means a lot to each of us.

We also want to thank Judy Wright, Jake Rondot, and others from the Human Kinetics team who believed in this project and made this publication a reality. The lives of many people are changed through decisions like yours.

My own role was initially as a facilitator and writer. As the scope of the project increased, my role also included being the grant writer, general manager, and editor. Informally I became known as "the SD" (Slave Driver). I look back on the list of amazing contributors, and I am reminded how each one of us can make a positive difference in this world. One person's enthusiasm (Marie) for helping children be active grew into an amazing web of people who produced this resource. To all of you, thank you. To you, the user of this resource, your thanks will come when you use these materials and ideas and you see happy smiles on the flushed faces of active participants. Each one of us makes a difference in the lives of those around us. Use your lives to make a difference for the good of all.

Thank you everyone! Now let's get moving!

John Byl
CIRA Ontario president

PART 1

GET READY!
Setting Up a Daily Physical Activity Program

Daily physical activity provides incredible benefits for children's well-being and academic success. Because you are using this resource, you are undoubtedly convinced of the many benefits of this kind of activity. Your energy and passion are well founded and are instrumental to the success of a daily physical activity (DPA) program.

However, if the burden of planning and implementing the entire program for your school falls on your shoulders, you are prone to burnout, and a great initiative goes down with you. For sustainability, DPA programs require broader support. Chapter 1 will help convince those not yet on board by outlining the background, legislation, and rationale behind DPA. To develop student leaders and engage the rest of the staff, consult chapter 2 for scheduling options and a step-by-step guide to implementing a DPA program. Chapter 2 also provides many other resources to further broaden your program.

With *Everybody Move!* in your hands, with the support of colleagues, and with the enthusiasm of some excited and trained students, implementation and sustainability of daily physical activity will be most rewarding. Let's get ready to move!

CHAPTER 1

Why Should Everybody Move?

The health of North American youth is decreasing at an alarming rate. Children and youth are more physically inactive than in past generations. We are facing an inactivity epidemic (CAHPERD 2006). Adults and children are not physically active enough to be healthy. An overemphasis on sedentary activities combined with high-calorie and low-quality food supports a future of obesity and other health concerns for children. Youth are at particular risk for becoming sedentary as they grow older. Because children spend most of their time in school, schools can play an important role in providing opportunities for enjoyable physical activity and encouraging children to adopt an active lifestyle.

PROMOTING DAILY PHYSICAL ACTIVITY IN SCHOOLS

A daily physical activity (DPA) program is an action plan to reverse current inactivity trends and improve or maintain children's overall health and wellness while enhancing their learning opportunities. With few physical education specialists in the schools and limited time and space, the challenge is to deliver DPA to all children in an effective way. However, "Schools have the responsibility of creating and nurturing a learning environment for students that supports the development of the life-long habit for daily physical activity for healthy lifestyles" (Shelley Barthel, Schools Come Alive 2005). Physical activity can be incorporated into the school day through physical education, elementary school recess, physical activity breaks, physical activity clubs, activities before and after school, activities during lunch hour, special events, and activities during other curricular subject time.

The characteristics of a DPA program vary with federal, state, and provincial legislation. The variations occur in the following areas:

- Free time or instructional time: For some students, DPA must be scheduled during instructional time and cannot include lunch time, recess, breaks, and activities before or after school. Other states and provinces accept time within the physical education program, before and after school, lunch time, recess, intramurals, and extracurricular activities toward the DPA requirement.

- Space: DPA may occur in classrooms, in gymnasiums, in hallways, in multi-purpose rooms, and outdoors.

- Length of time: Time required to fulfill DPA ranges from 20 to 60 minutes. Some schools permit DPA to occur in several short sessions (minimum of 10 minutes each) over the course of the school day.
- Intensity: Some states and provinces require moderate or vigorous activity, while others encourage any kind of movement. During moderate activity, there is some increase in breathing and heart rate while the person can talk comfortably. Vigorous activity involves increases in breathing and heart rate and may cause puffing. The person can talk, but carrying on a conversation may be difficult.
- Inclusion: All districts emphasize that activities must be adapted, where appropriate, to ensure that students with special needs can participate. Such adaptations must be consistent with accommodations or modifications that are typically found in a student's IEP (individualized education plan in the United States, individual education plan in Canada).

This resource provides planning and implementation ideas that leaders can use to create a daily physical activity program that everyone can enjoy, from school children to senior citizens.

DISTINGUISHING PHYSICAL ACTIVITY FROM PHYSICAL EDUCATION

Physical education and *physical activity* are two terms often used synonymously with each other; however, although they are connected, they have different meanings. The National Association for Sport and Physical Education (NASPE) defines *physical activity* as any movement form that contributes to the development and maintenance of good health. Physical education seeks to develop persons who have the knowledge, skills, and confidence to enjoy a lifetime of healthful physical activity. Quality physical education is foundational for a successful daily physical activity program because of its role in helping students gain the knowledge and skills to become proficient movers and participants in a lifetime of physical activity.

NASPE has developed national standards for a successful physical education program (2006). A physically educated person does the following:

1. Demonstrates competency in motor skills and movement patterns needed for performing a variety of physical activities
2. Demonstrates understanding of movement concepts, principles, strategies, and tactics as they apply to the learning and performance of physical activities
3. Participates regularly in physical activity
4. Achieves and maintains a health-enhancing level of physical fitness
5. Exhibits responsible personal and social behavior that respects self and others in physical activity settings
6. Values physical activity for health, enjoyment, challenge, self-expression, or social interaction

These standards provide a framework for the development of a quality physical education program and set realistic and achievable expectations for all students.

NASPE (2004) has also developed guidelines for physical activity for children from birth to 12 years. Following are the guidelines for school-aged children (5-12 years):

1. Children should accumulate at least 60 minutes of age-appropriate physical activity on all or most days of the week. This daily accumulation should include moderate and vigorous physical activity, with the majority of the time being spent in intermittent activities.

2. Children should participate in several bouts of physical activity lasting 15 minutes or more each day.

3. Children should participate each day in a variety of age-appropriate physical activities designed to achieve optimal health, wellness, fitness, and performance benefits.

4. Extended periods (periods of two hours or more) of inactivity are discouraged for children, especially during the daytime hours.

In 2008, the U.S. Department of Health and Human Services further encouraged physical activity through the Physical Activity Guidelines for Americans (U.S. Department of Health and Human Services 2008a). The guidelines recommend that children and adolescents be active for at least one hour a day for at least three days a week at a moderate or vigorous aerobic level. Children and adolescents should also incorporate muscle-strengthening and bone-strengthening activities three times a week.

COMPREHENSIVE SCHOOL PHYSICAL ACTIVITY PROGRAM (CSPAP)

In 2004, U.S. federal legislation (Public Law 108-265) was passed requiring all districts with federally funded school lunch programs to develop and implement wellness policies, including the setting of goals for physical activity by the beginning of the 2006-2007 school year. Districts were to engage in a wide range of policy development and have a plan for measuring policy implementation. Implementation of these wellness plans was expected to result in an increase in school-based opportunities for physical activity.

In recognition of the increasing youth obesity problem, the need arose for the development and implementation of a comprehensive approach to enhance both physical education and physical activity in schools at the state, district, and school level. The National Association for Sport and Physical Education (2008) recommends that all PK-12 schools implement a comprehensive school physical activity program (CSPAP). The CSPAP encompasses physical activity programming before, during, and after the school day and includes quality physical education; school-based physical activity opportunities; school employee wellness and involvement; and family and community involvement.

The objective outlined in the CSPAP for school-based physical activity opportunities is for children to reach the recommended 60 minutes of physical activity each day. The school-based physical activity opportunities would supplement time accumulated during physical education class and allow students to use the skills and knowledge learned in physical education to successfully be active. For elementary students, recess can be used to provide opportunities for physical activity.

NASPE recommends at least one daily period of recess for a minimum of 20 minutes. For middle school students, allowing free time for drop-in activities—such as at a fitness center—is encouraged. Programming before and after school, lunch hour intramurals, and interscholastic programs may also be included in the 60 minutes of physical activity per child per day.

An equally important benefit of physical activity is the increase in academic achievement of many students. Students need physical activity breaks from sedentary activities in the classroom. Integrating physical activity in the school day may enhance academic performance. Sedentary classroom activities should be interspersed with physical activity breaks, and movement should be integrated into the academic content when possible. This resource focuses on school-based physical activity opportunities outside of physical education, although many of the activities can also be used within a physical education lesson.

MAKING THE CASE FOR DPA PROGRAMS

Many excellent DPA programs exist to meet the needs of administrators, teachers, and children. Canada, Australia, and the United States have launched similar successful programs to incorporate daily physical activity in schools to improve the health of students. Characteristics of each program are presented to provide an understanding of the breadth and scope of DPA.

DPA Programs in Canada

Canada has been at the forefront of developing DPA programs. Education in Canada is provincially governed, and as a result several outstanding provincial programs have emerged. Health Canada recommends that children work up to 90 minutes of daily physical activity, and decrease daily screen time by 90 minutes.

Ontario

In 2005, the Ontario health and physical education curriculum was revised to require a minimum of 20 minutes of sustained moderate to vigorous activity each day. Students are expected to participate vigorously on a regular basis in a wide range of physical activities. An activity deemed vigorous raises the heart rate and maintains this increase for an uninterrupted period of time. DPA is incorporated into the instructional day in a variety of ways. It is built into existing physical education classes or scheduled as additional classes on days when students do not already have a health and physical education period.

Alberta

In September 2005, the Government of Alberta mandated a requirement of 30 minutes of daily physical activity for all students in grades 1 to 9 based on the belief that healthy students are better able to learn and that school communities should provide supportive environments for students to develop positive habits needed for a healthy, active lifestyle.

The conditions proposed for meeting daily physical activity requirements in Alberta differ from those in Ontario. All students must be physically active for a minimum of 30 minutes daily through any type of activity that is organized by the school. DPA should be offered in as large a block of time as possible but can also be offered in time segments adding up to the minimum 30 minutes per day (e.g., two 15-minute blocks of time). DPA should be incorporated throughout the day and integrated into other subject areas.

British Columbia

Effective September 2008, British Columbia requires all K-12 students to participate in 30 minutes of physical activity per day during either instructional or noninstructional school time. Students in grades 10 to 12 must document and report a minimum of 150 minutes per week of physical activity, at a moderate to vigorous intensity, as part of their graduation requirements. Under the banner of "every move is a good move," British Columbia developed the DPA Action Tracker as an interactive tool for students in grades 10 to 12 (British Columbia Ministry of Education 2009). The Action Tracker enables students to keep track of their daily physical activities and create a printed report for their teacher or school administrator.

DPA Programs in Australia

The Government of Queensland, Australia, through the Get Active Queensland Children and Young People strategy, encourages regular physical activity to address growing levels of childhood obesity. The Smart Moves initiative, which promotes physical activity programs in Queensland state schools, has produced several outstanding resources for teachers (Queensland Government 2008). The Smart Moves program was developed to increase the curriculum time students are engaged in physical activity at school and to improve the quality of that activity. All primary schools must allocate 30 minutes per day of physical activity of at least moderate intensity as part of the school curriculum. All secondary schools are required to provide at least two hours of physical activity each school week at moderate intensity during curriculum time for lower secondary school students.

DPA Programs in the United States

Several states have implemented programs to increase physical activity. These states include Texas, New Hampshire, Delaware, Connecticut, and New York.

Texas

The Texas Department of State Health Services developed the Nutrition, Physical Activity and Obesity Prevention Program. Part of this program, developed in conjunction with the City of Fort Worth, contains a physical activity curriculum titled Getting Fit Texas! (2008). The program encourages participants of all ages to accumulate at least 30 minutes of activity most days of the week and to try to build up to 60 minutes of activity to achieve or maintain a healthy weight.

New Hampshire

In spring 2008, New Hampshire developed a new state rule to support daily physical activity. Each local school must adopt a written policy about physical activity. The school policy recommends that all students in elementary school through high school participate in developmentally appropriate physical activity and exercise for a minimum of 30 minutes each day. Practices suggested for the policy include walking programs, family fitness programs, integrating health and physical activity across the school curriculum, and physical activity recess periods (New Hampshire Department of Education 2009).

Delaware

In 2008, House Bill 372 was passed requiring each school district and charter school in Delaware to assess the physical condition of each student at least once in grades K to 5, 6 to 8, and 9 to 12, with results to be provided to parents, guardians, or relative caregivers. The Fitnessgram was chosen by the Department of Education as the assessment tool for determining the physical fitness of each student. House Bill 471 also created a pilot program to determine the best practices and assessment that could be implemented in schools statewide for physical education and physical activity. Nineteen schools were selected for the pilot program (Delaware Department of Education 2007).

Connecticut

In *Action Guide for School Nutrition and Physical Activity Policies*, the Connecticut State Department of Education proposed several important recommendations regarding physical activity in schools. First, school districts will provide students with a variety of opportunities for daily physical activity and quality physical education. All students in grades K-12, including students with disabilities and special health care needs and in alternative educational settings, shall receive daily physical education (150 minutes per week for elementary school students and 225 minutes per week for middle and high school students) for the entire school year. The action plan recommends that a certified physical education teacher teach all the physical education classes. Elementary school recess must be at least 20 minutes a day, preferably outdoors, during which schools should encourage moderate to vigorous physical activity and provide space, equipment, and an environment that is conducive to safe and enjoyable activity. For students to receive the nationally recommended amount of daily physical activity (at least 60 minutes per day) and to fully embrace regular physical activity as a personal behavior, students need opportunities for physical activity beyond physical education class. Physical activity can easily be incorporated into the classroom, as part of the learning process or as an energizing break. Finally, the action plan states that classroom teachers shall provide short physical activity breaks between lessons or classes, as appropriate.

New York

New York State Education Law requires schools to provide opportunities for all students to learn and develop the skills, knowledge, and attitudes necessary to participate in a lifetime of healthful physical activity. Recently, New York State adopted a model approach for promoting healthy eating and physical activity in schools. Elements of the model approach include strengthening or creating a representative school-based team at the building level, which may include teachers, staff, parents, administrators, students, and community members; developing a district health advisory council; and collecting data from each school to determine strengths and challenges. New

York State launched Activ8Kids! in June 2005 to fight childhood obesity and promote healthy lifestyles among children. One of the resources created to assist schools is *Activ8Kids! New York State School Nutrition and Physical Activity Best Practices Toolkit.*

CHILDREN AND PHYSICAL INACTIVITY— FACTS AND STATS

Daily physical activity offers many benefits. This section provides facts and statistics that you can use to support your program by including the information in newsletters, posting it on your bulletin boards, or distributing it in any other way that encourages your school to get moving.

Healthy Benefits of Physical Activity

When patterns of physical activity are started at a young age, the impact can be lasting. The U.S. Department of Health and Human Services (1996) reports the following:

- Moderate daily physical activity can reduce the risk of developing cardiovascular disease, type 2 diabetes, and certain cancers. Daily physical activity helps lower blood pressure and cholesterol; helps prevent or retard osteoporosis; and helps reduce obesity, symptoms of anxiety and depression, and symptoms of arthritis.
- Heart disease is the leading cause of death among men and women in the United States. Physically inactive people are twice as likely to develop coronary heart disease than are regularly active people.
- The benefits of active lifestyles include improved mood and feelings of well-being; better control of body weight, blood glucose, blood pressure, and cholesterol; health benefits for people who have chronic diseases or disabilities; and increased quality of life for all persons.

Following are some other supported health benefits of physical activity:

- Has a positive effect on type 2 diabetes (Tudor-Locke, Bell, and Myers 2000)
- Increases bone mineral density (Drowatzky and Drowatzky 2000)
- Helps restore overall health to obese children (Hunter, Gamman, and Hester 2000)
- Decreases probability of smoking (Statistics Canada 2001)
- Contributes to increased life span and lowered rates of heart disease (Froelicher and Froelicher 1991; Paffenbarger, Hyde, and Dow 1991)
- Improves self-esteem and self-concept in children and contributes to a reduction in depressive symptoms, stress, and anxiety (McKay et al. 1996)
- Enhances social and moral development (Shields and Bredemeier 1994)
- Provides opportunities for the development of leadership skills; participants develop camaraderie, character, and sense of fair play (Byl 2002)
- Has a positive effect on academic achievement; "studies indicate that children between the ages of four and nine who participate in physical activities tend to have fewer difficulties in reading and math and have developed better study habits than those who rarely participate" (Statistics Canada 2001)

- Is useful in creating a positive school culture and decreasing vandalism and as a positive intervention strategy for behavior management (Norrie and Mustard 1999)

In recent years there has been an alarming increase in the number of overweight children and youth, in part because not enough young people are engaging in regular physical activity. Time spent on physical education in schools is lacking, even though physical activity has been shown to improve academic performance. The following studies support these claims.

Overweight Among Youth

- Sixteen percent of children and teens aged 6 to 19 were overweight in the years 1999 to 2002, triple the proportion in 1980. Fifteen percent of children in the same age group are considered at risk for becoming overweight. The percentage of overweight African American, Hispanic, and Native American children is about 20 percent (U.S. Department of Health and Human Services 2009).
- More than 10 percent of children between the ages of 2 and 5 are overweight, double the proportion since 1980 (U.S. Department of Health and Human Services 2009).
- Approximately 60 percent of obese American children aged 5 to 10 have at least one cardiovascular disease risk factor such as elevated total cholesterol, triglycerides, insulin, or blood pressure, and 25 percent have two or more risk factors (Freedman et al. 1999).
- Forty percent of Canadian children already have at least one risk factor for heart disease (Fishburne and Harper-Tarr 1992).
- Children and adolescents who are overweight by the age of 8 are 80 percent more likely to become overweight or obese adults (NASPE 2006).
- The percentage of American children aged 6 to 11 who are overweight has more than tripled over the past 30 years (Howe and Freedson 2008).
- In 2004, twenty-six percent of Canadian children and adolescents aged 2 to 17 were overweight or obese (Shields 2006).
- Twenty-five percent of Australian school-aged boys and 23 percent of girls were classified as overweight or obese (Booth et al. 2006).

Physical Activity by Young People

- More than one-third of American young people in grades 9 to 12 do not regularly engage in vigorous physical activity (Grunbaum et al. 2004).
- One-third of American young people in grades 9 to 12 participate in an insufficient amount of moderate to vigorous physical activity (Grunbaum et al. 2004).
- The proportion of adolescents in grades 9 through 12 who engaged regularly in vigorous physical activity (lasting at least 20 minutes on three or more of the previous seven days that made the student sweat or breathe hard) was 64 percent in 2007. There has been little change in the proportion since 1999. The Healthy People 2010 goal is 85 percent for this age group (U.S. Department of Health and Human Services 2008b).
- Overall, among American high school students, males are more physically active than females. White students are more active than black and Hispanic students (Grunbaum et al. 2004).
- Physical activity declines as children get older: 1- to 4-year-olds are active approximately 25 hours per week, 5- to 12-year-olds are active approximately 18 hours per week, and 13- to 17-year-olds are active approximately 15 hours per week (Canadian Fitness and Lifestyle Research Institute 1995).

- According to the 2000-2001 Canadian Community Health Survey (CCHS), 56 percent of Canadian youth aged 12 to 19 were physically inactive. However, as many as 82 percent may not have been active enough to meet international guidelines for optimal growth and development (www.cflri.ca).
- Canadian girls are significantly less active than boys, with 64 percent of girls and 48 percent of boys being considered physically inactive (Stats Canada 2003).
- American children and youth in low income and single-parent families face increased barriers to physical activity (The President's Council 1997).

School Physical Education

- The percentage of students who attended a daily physical education class has dropped from 42 percent in 1991 to 28 percent in 2003 (Centers for Disease Control and Prevention 2004).
- Only 4 percent of American elementary schools provide daily physical education throughout the school year (NASPE 2006).
- Less than one-fifth of Canadian children between the ages of 6 and 12 take part in daily physical education (CFLRI–Physical Activity Monitor 2002).

Physical Activity and Academic Performance

- Physical activity has a positive effect on academic performance (Tomporowski et al. 2007).
- Positive associations between physical activity and cognitive function, particularly for executive function, are supported. Executive function is the ability to plan and select activities to organize goal-directed action and promote decision-making skills. Executive function is essential for psychological and social development in children (Ethnier et al. 2006).
- "Students who participated in an aerobics (daily running) program achieved higher levels in reading, language and mathematics and had better cardiovascular fitness" (Centers for Disease Control and Prevention 1997).
- Researchers demonstrate the positive effects daily physical activity has on student academic achievement and performance in the areas of memory, observation, problem-solving and decision-making, as well as significant improvements in attitudes, discipline, behaviors, and creativity (Keays and Allison 1995).

SUMMARY

The challenge of improving the health of children and youth through physical activity is significant. Providing developmentally appropriate opportunities for children to be active and have fun is the essential goal of this book. Your initiative to take on DPA will make your life and the lives of children much richer. Everybody will be healthier and more active. Chapter 2 will help you begin this challenge by presenting options for organizing your DPA program and a step-by-step guide to implementing a DPA program. Chapter 2 also provides many other resources to further strengthen your program.

Developing a Daily Physical Activity Program

Although most people support the need for daily physical activity in schools as mandated by provincial, state, or federal curriculum policies, starting a school DPA program can be a daunting task. Ensuring that both students and staff are able to participate in the required amount of daily physical activity is the challenge. Where to begin? Several steps and methods for developing and implementing a successful DPA program are presented in this chapter. Many schools have found that a combination of methods works best for meeting their needs.

To make DPA happen and to build sustainability into the program, the organization of DPA needs to be bigger than yourself. You need to surround yourself with lots of good people, develop broad ownership for DPA, and dream big. To reach your dreams, you will need to set attainable goals and plan to celebrate their completion. The three steps that follow and the rest of the chapter help you make DPA a long-term success.

NASPE (2006) outlines three steps to begin your DPA program:

Step 1: Appoint a leadership team to develop and oversee DPA in your school. Involve everyone who can help facilitate the school's plan.

Step 2: Involve the school employees as well as students' families and the community.

Step 3: Create a vision statement and action plan appropriate to the specific school, addressing components of the comprehensive school physical activity program (CSPAP). The action plan should include the baseline assessment; objectives and activities to meet each objective; defined outcomes; timelines; and persons responsible for each component area.

SETTING UP THE ACTION PLAN FOR DAILY PHYSICAL ACTIVITY

There are various approaches for conducting a baseline assessment of the CSPAP components as they currently exist in the school. The component areas are as follows:

- Quality physical education
- Before-school strategies

- During-school strategies
- After-school strategies
- Staff personal wellness

IMPLEMENTING DAILY PHYSICAL ACTIVITY

Daily physical activity programs can be implemented in various ways within a school. Each approach has advantages and disadvantages. Schools may choose a method of implementation based on the number of students and the resources available to them. The following are some of the methods a school may use to set up its own daily physical activity program (CAHPERD 2006a).

Daily Physical Education

Physical activity is a major component of a quality physical education program (Ontario Education 2006). There are many advantages to this option. One of the reasons students may not receive the recommended minutes of physical activity is that classroom teachers may not have the knowledge or confidence to implement the program themselves. If students have scheduled daily physical education, classroom teachers may be less apprehensive about a daily physical activity program. Also, because physical activity time takes place during physical education, there is often greater flexibility in activity options. Students are exposed to more variety and may find an activity they will continue to pursue and enjoy throughout their lives. There are also some downfalls to this method of DPA implementation. This program produces the best results if led by a qualified physical education teacher. Often many schools, especially elementary, do not have the resources to hire a full-time physical education teacher. Also, scheduling physical education for all classes every day may prove to be difficult, especially if the school does not have sufficient facilities or has a large number of students enrolled; however, if schools have flexible timetabling options and fewer students, this option has potential to be very successful.

Schoolwide DPA

Some schools schedule a block of physical activity for the participation of the entire school. Schoolwide DPA involves the entire school in physical activity at the same time. The activities can be completed in 10-minute blocks or in one time frame. How the program works is to have five different 10- to 20-minute activities or routines, one for each day of the week. The variety helps keep students motivated. The music and instruction is played over the public address (PA) system at a designated time each day, and teachers or student leaders can lead the program. The routines can be changed two or three times a year for variety. DPA can be scheduled immediately before a break in the day (e.g., recess, lunch), allowing students to use the break time to freshen up, change, hydrate, and refuel.

Schools have several options when choosing to implement a schoolwide daily physical activity program. The first option is for the physical activity to take place in all classrooms after announcements (Ontario Education 2006). A second option is to take a few minutes from each period throughout the day and accumulate them at the end of the day for physical activity. In the third option, the entire school performs an activity together outside or in the gymnasium at a regularly scheduled time (Ontario Education 2006). Staff, student leaders, and community specialists can lead the students. The scheduled time for the physical activity can be rotated throughout the week to prevent the same subject being affected by the decreased time. DPA can also be part of special school events, such as celebrations or theme days (Ontario Education 2006).

With a commonly scheduled time and the entire school involved, everyone is ensured of participation, and only one master copy of the music is required in the office.

Choosing to organize schoolwide DPA provides students with the opportunity to receive more than the minimum of daily physical activity on the days they have physical education class. Schools may invite guest presenters or members from the community to help with the program, promoting important relationships between students and the community. A schoolwide physical activity program also presents the opportunity for increased parental involvement. Despite its many benefits, some schools may find a schoolwide physical activity program difficult to coordinate and schedule. Some school staff may not consider a schoolwide program as important as other subject areas. Some schools may not have the facilities or resources to allow all students and staff to participate together in one location. Despite these disadvantages, a schoolwide DPA program ensures all students can participate in an active, healthy lifestyle.

Individual Classroom DPA With Cross-Curricular Links

DPA can also be led by the classroom teacher either during a schoolwide time period or at a time set by the individual teacher. The classroom teacher can establish strong cross-curricular links between DPA and other subjects so that DPA can be appropriately scheduled within another subject's allocated time period (e.g., teaching a folk dance in social studies). Physical activity can be done in the classroom, out of doors, or in other open spaces. Integration of physical activity and other subjects can help develop learning experiences for the students, enhance fitness and health, and provide an opportunity for educational exchange and discovery. When students see that physical activity can be integrated into all aspects of their lives, they are more likely to remember and appreciate physical activity on their own.

There are several advantages to this method of DPA. First, because physical activity can be done in any space at any time during the day, this method is easier to schedule into a school day. Secondly, students can experience hands-on opportunities to develop understanding of curriculum and link their knowledge to other concepts (Ontario Education 2006). Physical activity can help increase information retention and cater to different learning styles (Alberta Education 2005). Cross-curricular linking can give more meaning to concepts and make learning fun (Alberta Education 2005). Third, teachers have control over the classroom scheduling and can schedule DPA to fit with the rest of the curriculum for the day.

Some teachers may not appreciate the importance of being physically active on a daily basis. When the classroom teacher is solely responsible for DPA time, rather than a schoolwide time, some teachers may be tempted to neglect DPA in favor of other school subjects. Also, because classroom teachers do not always have a physical education background, they may not believe they have the knowledge or skills to think of classroom activities. Finally, because physical activity in the classroom can be linked with other subject areas, students may not receive an adequate warm-up or cool-down, which are important components of a daily physical activity program and of teaching students how to live a healthy lifestyle.

Creative DPA Combinations

Some schools have enjoyed success with DPA programs by combining several options throughout the year as follows:

- Schoolwide DPA is held for 10 minutes, and individual classroom teachers allocate additional blocks of DPA during homeroom time.
- DPA is scheduled into different facilities (e.g., a specific hallway where classes can participate in a fitness circuit).

- Partners or group classes share a facility appropriate for larger numbers of students, rather than trying to find individual facilities for each class.

- Two classes come together to form "fitness buddies." One older class teams up with one younger class. Senior students learn DPA activities in physical education class and are trained as leaders for the younger class. Older and younger classes meet to do a variety of different activities together both in the classroom and outside. Activities could include playground games, classroom dance routines, aerobics, or mixed-grade team mini-games such as four-goal soccer. The activities need to be changed regularly to maintain interest. The space needs to be big enough for two classes.

- Once a week, a time is designated during the school day for a whole-school or multigrade activity (e.g., fitness walk around school yard, line dance, circuits).

Intramural and Active Recess Programs

Many schools conduct intramural programs during lunch hour or before or after school hours. The active recess program is an excellent example discussed in the daily physical activity handbook distributed by Alberta Education (2005). There are many advantages to an active recess program. Students engage in increased physical activity and gain the opportunity to develop movement and manipulative skills. Also, interaction among students during physical activity can promote fair play, cooperation, respect for others, and a reduction in bullying (Alberta Education 2005). Students are encouraged to be creative and develop their problem-solving skills as well.

Active recess and intramural programs can promote multiculturalism and respect for diversity (Alberta Education 2005). A disadvantage is that both programs are often optional for students. There is no way teachers can monitor whether each child is receiving the recommended amount of physical activity. Intramural programs also present challenges in organization and finding staff or parent volunteers to supervise activities, especially before or after school. Despite these challenges, intramural and active recess programs have potential for success because they can offer students a variety of activities and give students choices in what activities they enjoy.

Different programs work for different schools. Start simple and build. Do not be afraid to make changes if things start to feel boring or do not seem to be working. It may take a while to get going. Be patient! Try, try again. It will be worth it!

ORGANIZING A DPA LEADERSHIP TEAM

A successful DPA program requires an effective leadership team. The purpose of the leadership team or committee is to plan and execute DPA and may include the training and development of student leaders. Determine who will be the DPA leader for each division within the school. As a team, decide how DPA should be delivered.

Creating a DPA Team or Committee

First, seek out staff members who are willing to provide leadership and are knowledgeable in the area of physical activity. Identify a team leader for your program. Teams and committees tend to function more effectively with a willing and capable chair or leader. This key contact person will lead, promote, organize, and delegate tasks within the DPA program. Your DPA team or committee leader should be someone who is

- a curriculum leader or who has experience in the areas of health and physical education,
- willing to organize and coordinate training opportunities for other teachers,
- willing to attend sessions and build connections with community partners,
- willing to seek out and apply for funding to support DPA (equipment grants, music resources), and
- an advocate of health and active living.

Second, schools can build on existing health and wellness committees, school councils, and advisory groups which may already be established within the school or community that has expertise in the area of physical education or physical activity.

Third, allow opportunities for other stakeholders to become involved, such as staff, students, parents, and community partners. To encourage the ownership and involvement of the entire staff, the DPA team can delegate the responsibility for organizing and leading the DPA sessions to divisions or grades for a short period of time.

Appointing Student Leaders

One effective way of implementing a daily physical activity program is to train DPA student leaders. Student leaders support teachers who are less keen or confident about physical activity. Student leaders provide relief in planning DPA activities for classroom teachers, motivate students, receive leadership skill development opportunities, and promote physical activity as role models. The following steps will assist schools in developing student leaders.

Step 1: Inform

Have an information and sign-up session for students interested in becoming daily physical activity leaders.

Step 2: Select Leaders

Select all potential leaders who show enthusiasm and commitment. Discuss expectations and the role of the leaders. Student leaders are expected to do the following:

- Attend all training sessions.
- Be a good role model.
- Be responsible to know which classroom they will be leading.
- Arrive at each class prepared to lead with running shoes and appropriate clothing.
- Pick up required materials (music and routines) before going to the class, if necessary.
- Lead activities in a safe and enthusiastic manner.
- Ensure that the activity area is safe for the participants and leaders.
- Attend all meetings for student leaders.

FIGURE 2.1 **Student Leader Commitment Form**

My schoolwork comes first so I will keep up with my class work and homework. To prepare for leading the activities, I will:

- Attend all meetings and training sessions for student leaders.
- Know which classroom I will be leading.
- Pick up required materials (music, routines, equipment) before going to the classroom.
- Arrive at each classroom with running shoes and appropriate clothing and prepared to lead.

When I lead, I will:

- Be an enthusiastic and positive role model.
- Ensure that the activity area is safe for everyone.
- Lead activities in a safe manner.
- Have fun and smile!

If I am unable to keep these promises, I realize I may be asked to give up my position as an activity leader.

Student leader's name (print): _____

Student leader's signature: _____

Supervisor's signature: _____

Date: _____

Based on P.A.L.S. (Playground Activity Leaders in Schools), Region of Peel.

- Keep up with class work and homework.
- Have fun and smile!

Student leaders should read and sign a commitment form (see figure 2.1 for an example).

Step 3: Train Leaders

Decide what days of the week and times of the day the training sessions will occur. Meeting three or four times a week is recommended to learn and practice routines and activities until the student leaders have the necessary skill level to lead a class.

Step 4: Group Leaders Into Teams

Pair leaders to work as a team. If there are too many, make groups of three students. It is intimidating for most students to lead on their own. Working with a partner distributes the pressure, and if one leader forgets a step, the other is likely to remember it. Using groups of three works well, because if one person is away there are always two leaders.

FIGURE 2.2	Daily Leader Schedule

Date: _____ to _____

Room #	Teacher	Leaders

Step 5: Schedule Activities

Scheduling is challenging and time consuming. A copy of every teacher's scheduled physical education times is needed in order to coordinate when the leaders go to each classroom. Make up a weekly and daily schedule indicating the room number and the leaders (see figures 2.2 and 2.3). This schedule should change every few weeks for variety.

Step 6: Organize Resources and Equipment

Keeping track of resources and equipment is essential for the successful implementation of a student-led DPA program. Numerous copies of the music and several sound systems for playing music are required. Keep your resources (books, videos, music) in a central location. Develop a system to manage them (e.g., signing out resources).

FIGURE 2.3	Sample Weekly Location Schedule

This location schedule indicates where the teacher's class will be during scheduled DPA time. In most elementary schools, the schedule can remain the same all year.

Key

M: Music room
G: Gymnasium
L: Library
F: French room

Classroom #	Teacher	Mon.	Tues.	Wed.	Thurs.	Fri.
1	Miss Brown	1	1	1	M	1
2	Mr. Singh	2	2	2	2	2
3	Ms. Green	F	3	3	3	G
4	Mrs. Pape	4	4	L	4	4

Suggestions vary, depending on which program model is used. Binders with activities and routines and equipment may be stored in each classroom, with a master copy of the music and additional resources kept in a designated area. Another option is for leaders to take a copy of the music, a copy of activities and routines, and equipment from a designated place to the room where they will be leading.

A successful DPA program can operate on limited equipment. Most of the activities in our resource require limited (if any) equipment, and you can use substitutions as long as everyone is having fun and being safe. You are free to use the equipment suggested or to use your creativity and create new ideas and tools. For the music component, some kind of sound system is required such as an MP3 player or CD player. The following is a list of equipment for an elementary DPA program. Select items that can make it easier for you to get everybody moving.

All Purpose

- Beanbags
- Skipping ropes
- Variety of balls (e.g., Gator Skin balls, Nerf balls, soccer balls, beach balls, basketballs, utility balls, tennis balls, Wiffle balls, footballs)
- Hoops
- Scooter boards
- Discs
- Pinnies or wristbands
- Flag football belts
- Pylons or floor markers

- Benches or chairs
- Floor mats
- Rubber chicken, rubber bass, or stuffed animals
- Sound system and music for motivation (e.g., the accompanying *Everybody Move!* CD)

Miscellaneous

- Stopwatches or timers
- Whistles
- Mesh bags
- Storage bins
- Plastic pails
- Floor tape
- Popsicle sticks for color-coding teams
- Plastic containers such as egg or jelly bean containers from dollar stores
- Rackets
- Shuttlecocks
- Scarves
- Grab bag with small miscellaneous objects such as Koosh balls and Hacky Sacks
- Trashballs (crumpled up newsprint placed in a shopping bag and taped on the outside for use like Hacky Sacks . . . only larger)

Step 7: Give Recognition

Leaders feel important if they are identifiable. Some possibilities for recognizing leaders include T-shirts that say "Daily Physical Activity Leader," sweatbands, caps, and armbands. Don't forget to acknowledge appreciation of student leaders at assemblies, at community events, and in the media.

FINDING SPACE FOR DPA

One of the most challenging aspects of DPA is finding space for student participation. Take an inventory of all the space available at your school for physical activity (classrooms, hallways, gymnasium, library, playground, concourse area), and plan activities to use all available space.

Be creative, and find ways to encourage students to be active outside too. Have a backup plan for days when weather is inclement (CAHPERD 2006b).

PLANNING AN ACTIVITY SESSION

The key to a successful DPA program is to take activity ideas that you hear about or read about and modify them to meet the needs of your students and space. Begin the session with a warm-up to gradually increase the students' heart rate and move joints through their range of motion. Use dynamic stretching such as controlled leg swings. Avoid static stretching (e.g., stretches that involve sitting down and holding a body part) in the warm-up.

Here are several important questions to ask when selecting activities for the DPA sessions:

- Is the activity continuous?
- Is the activity inclusive? Can all participate?
- Are large muscles moving to get heart rates up?
- Are there modifications to increase or decrease intensity?
- Are the participants engaged?
- Are the participants having fun?
- Do the participants know why they are doing the activities?

End the DPA session with a cool-down to gradually decrease the students' heart rates; develop flexibility through stretching; and relax with long, slow, deep breathing.

Planning an entire week of DPA sessions becomes easier with experience and support. Figure 2.4 gives an example of a weekly activity schedule.

FIGURE 2.4 **Sample Weekly Activity Schedule**

One Week of Quality Daily Fitness at Robert Little Public School

"It's time for Active School Challenge!"

"Let's get active, Robert Little!"

"Active bodies equal active minds!"

Monday

1. The Hustle (music and routine to "Marching Circus" from *Everybody Move!*)
2. Principal's Coming Activity (music: "Be True to Your School"*)
3. Latinique (music and routine from *Everybody Move!*)

Tuesday

1. Cha-Cha Slide (follow directions on song)
2. Fitness Circuit and Fitness Shake-Up Activities (music: "Rock Shot" from *Everybody Move!*)
3. Eddie the Razor (music and routine from *Everybody Move!*)

Wednesday

1. Hands Up (song and routine)
2. Fortune Cookie Fitness Activity (music: "Rock and Roll"*)
3. Ethno Tension (music and routine from *Everybody Move!*)

Thursday

1. Follow the Leader (The Soca Boys) (follow directions on song)
2. Poker Card Run Activity (music: "Mission Improbable"*)
3. Kokomo (The Beach Boys) (routine from *Everybody Move!*)

Friday

1. Hampsterdance (routine from *Everybody Move!*)
2. Winner's Olympics Activity (music: "Stadium Rock"*)
3. Eddie the Razor (music and routine from *Everybody Move!*)

*Or any upbeat music.

LEADING AN ACTIVITY

Once you have selected the activities for a DPA session, it is time to lead the students. Here are some helpful hints to make your session a success.

- Stick to common classroom management routines. Establish a signal for stopping and starting activities (e.g., a whistle, drum, handclap), and practice using it. Consider using both an auditory and visual signal, and whenever possible, write directions and expectations on a chalkboard or whiteboard.

- Divide the students into teams or groups first before explaining the activity.

- Place students at their starting areas.

- Give specific rules for the activity.

- Repeat the instructions as the activity progresses.

- Be a great role model. Participate on the perimeter of the activity space, which will allow you to see and supervise all students at all times.

Be creative. There is always more than one way to lead an activity to foster success, cooperation, and fun as well as challenge the abilities of all participants. Students can create wonderful activities, so be sure to allow opportunity for their input and ideas.

PROMOTING SAFETY

Plan and implement activity sessions that keep your students both physically and emotionally safe. Consider the following points:

- When doing activities in a room, there must be enough space in front of and behind each participant. Move desks and furniture if necessary.

- Ensure that all participants feel emotionally safe and can participate in a meaningful way.

- Encourage students to take care of each other and take responsibility for their actions, which in turn will create a safe activity environment.

- Be inclusive; modify activities if necessary in order to include everyone.

- Identify safe areas where students can stop to tie shoelaces, stretch, or catch their breath.

- Reinforce the importance of stopping on the side as opposed to in the middle of the activity space. Be sure to identify boundaries and danger zones where obstacles exist.

- To have students move safely in a limited amount of space, consider having students stand on two small pieces of carpet (scraps available from a carpet store) and move by shuffling along; or have students walk heel to toe, with the toe of one foot bumping into the heel of the other.

- Refer to national, state, and provincial safety guidelines and your school board guidelines. The following are URLs for safety resources:

- Ontario Physical Education Safety Guidelines (www.ophea.net/safety .cfm)
- Safety Guidelines for Physical Activity in Alberta Schools (www.ei.educ .ab.ca/documents/resources/safety_guidelines_2003.pdf)
- Health, Mental Health and Safety Guidelines for Schools (www.national guidelines.org/toc.cfm)
- Pennsylvania Department of Education Academic Standards for Health, Safety and Physical Education (www.pde.state.pa.us/stateboard_ed/lib/ stateboard_ed/sandyhealth.pdf)

ENSURING INCLUSION

The goal of this resource is to provide programs where everybody can move. For some students with special needs, DPA can be challenging but also enriching. Here are some guidelines for adapting physical activities:

- Consult directly with the person with the exceptionality. He knows best about his disability and what strategies can be developed to make him feel comfortable. Ask lots of questions, and make sure the participant is involved in every step of the inclusion process.
- Make adjustments to the activity only when necessary. Adaptations should aim to increase the person's participation, success, and enjoyment. Allow the participant to inform you of her needs.
- Approach inclusion on an individual basis. Certain adaptations are necessary for specific exceptionalities. Do not approach adaptations using general strategies. This can lead to making unsuitable and redundant adjustments.
- Reduce new skills down to their smallest components. This allows a participant to master each new skill component and build his skill set in a progressive fashion.
- Be fair. Any modifications to the activity should be fair to all participants involved regardless of ability. Modifications that single out students with disabilities only contribute to isolation and reinforce stereotypes.

Make sure equipment is available. If adaptations are based on specific equipment, and that equipment is not available, this may limit the participant's opportunities to get involved (CAHPERD 2006a).

RESOURCES

There is an abundance of resources for DPA. Following are some of our favorites.

Web Sites

These Web sites are useful resources to peruse in an effort to further enhance your program. Additional helpful activities and teacher resources are included. See the description by each Web site to get a quick idea of the tools available.

Canadian Provincial Government Sites— Excellent Ideas, Handbooks, and Activities

Alberta: www.education.gov.ab.ca/ipr/DailyPhysAct.asp

Alberta: www.education.gov.ab.ca/k_12/curriculum/bysubject/dpa.asp

British Columbia: www.healthservices.gov.bc.ca/cpa/mediasite/actnow.html

Nova Scotia: www.gov.ns.ca/ohp/physicalActivity/activeKidsHealthyKids.asp

Ontario: www.edu.gov.on.ca/eng/teachers/dpa.html

Ophea Teacher Resources and Activities:

www.ophea.net/Ophea/Ophea.net/teacherresources.cfm. This Web site provides links to the Ontario Ministry of Education curriculum as well as to health and physical education curriculum support. The Web site allows the user to do a broad search of any category or a more specific search by grade level and area of interest. The site provides titles of books, publishing and ordering information, abstracts, and reviews of books.

www.ophea.net/Ophea/Ophea.net/activityideas.cfm. This Web site provides a list of various fun activities to be used in the school. Each activity is clearly laid out with a list of required materials, a description of the activity, and an overview.

United States Education Sites—Action Plans and Activities

Activ8kids! New York State School Nutrition and Physical Activity Best Practices Toolkit (www.health.state.ny.us/prevention/obesity/activ8kids). This toolkit provides guidance and resources for promoting healthy eating and physical activity to school administrators, teachers, parents, and community partners.

Brain Breaks: A Physical Activity Idea Book for Elementary Classroom Teachers, Michigan Department of Education 2005 (www.emc.cmich.edu/brainbreaks).

Energizers, North Carolina University (www.ncpe4me.com/energizers.html).

Mind and Body: Activities for the Elementary Classroom, Montana Office of Public Instruction 2003 (www.opi.state.mt.us/PDF/health/Mind&Body.pdf).

Take 10! International Life Sciences Institute (ILSI) Center for Health Promotion. Ordering information at www.take10.net/whatistake10.asp.

Australian Resource

Daily Physical Activity Guide for Schools (www.sportrec.qld.gov.au/Publications/DailyPhysicalActivityGuideforSchools.aspx). An excellent comprehensive guide on how to develop a DPA program, including practical ideas to incorporate daily activity into other subjects without adding extra work for teachers; how to organize games and activities; and how to promote your program.

Physical Activity Sites

Canada's Physical Activity Guides for Children and Youth (www.phac-aspc .gc.ca/pau-uap/paguide/child_youth). Check out Canada's physical activity guides for further details and helpful information.

Active Living Rewards (www.activelivingrewards.ca). To assist older students and adults, you may want to encourage them to record their activities online and potentially win things for their activity.

Kidnetic.com (www.kidnetic.com). A great movement Web site with lots of neat information on exercise and nutrition for kids and parents. You can find fun activities, including an active fitness challenge on this site. The move-mixer section is handy, as you can move to preset dances or arrange them on your own.

CIRA Ontario (www.ciraontario.com). Access information about CIRA Ontario's many great resources. Active Playgrounds, You're It, Dances Even I Would Do, Bang for Your Buck, Oodles of Noodles, Why Paper and Scissors Rock, and

50 Games With 50 Tennis Balls are just a few of the CIRA Ontario resources that you could use to get people moving and having fun.

PE Central (www.pecentral.org). This Web site is designed for health and physical education teachers, parents, and students. It provides the latest information about developmentally appropriate physical education programs for children and youth. The site also provides a database of lesson plans and assessment ideas.

p.e.links4u (www.pelinks4u.org). This Web site promotes active and healthy lifestyles. Sections include adapted physical education; coaching and sports; elementary physical education; health, fitness, and nutrition; interdisciplinary physical education; secondary physical education; and technology in physical education. At the bottom of the homepage, you can sign up to receive a free monthly e-mailed digest of the p.e.links4u Web site sections and an update of the latest physical education news.

Suitable Songs

Music is a natural way to get people excited about moving. These lists include some great songs that motivate people to get up and move. These songs will be an excellent complement to this resource and to your fitness program. You can use the music however it is most useful. We have provided some suggestions.

Suggested Songs to Energize Your Participants

- "Macarena"
- "YMCA"
- "Cotton-Eyed Joe"
- "Hokey Pokey"
- "The Hustle"
- "Lollipop"
- "Men in Black" (Will Smith)
- "I Will Survive"
- "Hampsterdance" (Hampton the Hampster)
- "Chicken Dance"
- "Be True to Your School" (Beach Boys)
- "Cha-Cha Slide"
- "Hands Up"
- "Shake Your Booty"
- "Follow the Leader" (The Soca Boys)
- "All Star"
- "Kokomo" (Beach Boys)
- "Mambo #5"
- "Who Let the Dogs Out"
- "Body Rock" (Terri and Rick, *The Healthy Hustle*)
- "Get Ready for This"
- "Bring It All Back" (S Club 7)
- "Reach" (S Club 7)
- "Agadoo"

- "Superman"
- "Feelin' Good"
- "Move This" (Technotronic)
- "The Electric Slide"
- "Hot, Hot, Hot"
- "Dance to the Music"
- "Rock Around the Clock"

The most engaging music for your students is probably the music they listen to. Have them bring in their own music. You will need to set some ground rules in terms of the kind of language you permit and references to sexuality and violence. You will probably need to preview the music. Students will understand pretty quickly what your standards are. A great place to purchase music is from www.itunes.com.

Video and DVD Resources

Video resources can enhance your activity program by providing additional ways to get your participants excited about moving. People of all ages will be excited to learn the dance moves and will be inspired to include daily physical activity as an important part of their day.

> *Fit Kids Classroom Workout DVD*, Human Kinetics Video ISBN 0-7360-3790-X, 800-465-7301. Includes four 5-minute workouts, two 10-minute workouts, plus a brief healthy message at the end of every exercise segment.
>
> *Sesame Street: Let's Make Music*, SONY Wonder, or purchase through your local video store. Explore the world of music and rhythm with your favorite Sesame Street characters, featuring the cast of Stomp.
>
> *Everybody Dance!* Wintergreen Learning Products (www.wintergreen.ca). Includes dances such as YMCA, The Loco-Motion, The Electric Slide, and Hot, Hot, Hot.

SUMMARY

Starting a DPA program is quite a challenge but very rewarding for your school, students, staff, and community. We have presented several options for organizing, scheduling, and staffing DPA programs. Several excellent Web sites and music resources are provided to support and encourage your program. Now that you are organized and ready to roll, let the fun and games and dancing begin. The games and dances are the fun part; the organization makes DPA work well and keeps it sustainable.

PART II

GET MOVING!
FUN FITNESS ACTIVITIES

Everybody will enjoy moving to these fun fitness activities. This section is divided into four chapters. Chapter 3 describes fun activities that can be done in a classroom or a room with chairs and furniture. Chapter 4 describes fun activities that can be done in gymnasiums, hallways, large rooms, and concourse areas. Outdoor activities involving open spaces and fresh air are covered in chapter 5. Finally, chapter 6 describes a series of fun activities that are linked together and focus on a particular theme.

To move safely in a limited space, see the safety considerations in chapter 2, page 23. Many activities can be adapted to work in several locations. Be creative. You can combine ideas in this chapter with those found in part III (especially the Funky Moves section). To help you find your favorite game or choose a game by available equipment, see the activity finder starting on page v.

CHAPTER 3

Fun Fitness Activities in the Classroom

Larger spaces are often not available for activity, and you need to make do with the space in your classroom when you create 10-minute fitness breaks in your schedule. The activities in this chapter can be done in your classroom.

Some of the games involve using the desks, such as Bicycle Races or Classroom Triathlon. Other games can be done in the aisles and be connected with other courses, as with Jumping Beans, Line Jump, Jump the Answer, Math Match, or Fitness Spelling. For some activities you benefit from a bit more space, and you can give leadership opportunities to the players, as in Pass the Bass. Yet other activities require the whole classroom as a creative play space, as in Animal Walks, Magnetic Force Field, Grab Bag Improvisation, Who's Coming? or Climbers and Sliders. Divide the classroom into two sides, and you can play Speed Simon Says or Healthy Simon Says. For a couple of activities, you will need to move the desks out of the way and use the chairs, such as in Classroom Foosball or Pinball.

When a classroom is the only location for physical activity, participants will still have fun and stay safe as long as a few guidelines are observed. Instead of running, players can move by putting their heels in front of their toes when they move or by putting their feet on paper (on carpeted floors) or on pieces of scrap carpet (on tiled floors).

PASS THE BASS

》OBJECTIVE

To have players lead different exercises

》PLAYERS

Groups of 5 to 12 are ideal

》EQUIPMENT

One rubber bass per group (A rubber chicken or another rubber animal, a beanbag, or a tennis ball can be used, but an animal makes the activity more fun.)

》SETUP

1. Players stand in a circle.
2. The leader takes the bass and throws it to anyone in the circle.

》INSTRUCTIONS

1. The person who is holding the bass does an activity to increase his heart rate, and everyone else in the class copies him, until the leader yells, "Pass the Bass!"
2. The player throws the bass to someone else in the circle, who selects a new activity.
3. Players continue doing the first player's activity until the second person begins the new activity.

Safety Tip

Be aware of any latex allergies if using a rubber fish.

》VARIATIONS

» Pass the Bass, Cool-Down and Stretch: Done in the same way as Pass the Bass but using slower activities and stretches.

» Pass the Bass, Class to Class: When the class has done activities for 15 minutes, the students pass the bass to another class, challenging those students to do the same. Soon the whole school will be passing the bass! Classes can choose whatever activity they would like to do to get moving while they have the bass.

» Musical Pass the Bass: When the music stops, whoever has the bass does a new activity.

LINE JUMP

» OBJECTIVE

To create jumping patterns over a line or two

» PLAYERS

Individual students or groups of any size

» EQUIPMENT

Masking tape or string to make lines, or use existing lines on the floor

» SETUP

1. Create lines beside desks or in an open area. Lines can be parallel or crossed in a *T* or an *X*.
2. Each player is given her own set of lines.

» INSTRUCTIONS

1. Players make up patterns for jumping over lines (e.g., straddle, cross, jump right, jump left, one foot, two feet). Players practice the patterns.
2. Players should keep the patterns simple at first and not overly active or they will not be able to sustain the activity.

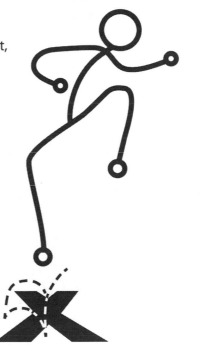

» SUGGESTED MUSIC

Choose music with a strong beat such as song 4 "Marching Circus" or song 21 "Stadium Rock."

» VARIATION

Group Line Jump: Encourage players to make up three different patterns on their lines that they can remember. The students then teach a partner, and the partners put their patterns together. Players can teach the group and create massive patterns and routines.

BICYCLE RACES

»» OBJECTIVE

For players to ride as long as possible

»» PLAYERS

Teams of two or three (teams of three work well)

»» EQUIPMENT

Two desks or tables placed closely together

»» SETUP

1. Divide the players into teams of two or three.
2. Each team pushes two desks close together with enough space between the desks for someone to stand.
3. Players stand in a line, with the first person standing between the two desks.

»» INSTRUCTIONS

1. On the signal to begin, the first player on each team puts his hands on the desks, lifts his legs, and starts to pedal as if riding a bike.
2. Teammates cheer and encourage.
3. When the rider cannot pedal anymore, he drops and moves to the back of the line. The second rider immediately "mounts the bike," and she begins to ride.

»» SUGGESTED MUSIC

Song 21 ("Stadium Rock") from the *Everybody Move!* CD.

Safety Tips

* Ensure desks are securely in place.
* Ensure teams are spaced far enough apart from each other.

»» VARIATIONS

»» Increase the speed; lean into corners; pretend to ride uphill or coast downhill.
»» Challenge teams to have a rider moving continuously so there is only a brief break between riders.
»» Players can also sit on a desk and hold onto it with their hands or place their hands on a desk and lift their legs to pedal.

JUMPING BEANS

» **OBJECTIVE**

For players to do the actions of the called-out beans

» **PLAYERS**

Any size group

» **EQUIPMENT**

A large chart listing the bean names and corresponding activity so players know which action to do when the bean name is called out (optional but helpful)

» **SETUP**

Teach the players the following "bean" shapes or actions.

- » Baked beans: Make your body as small as possible.
- » Broad beans: Make your body into a wide shape.
- » Pinto bean: Pretend to ride a pony!
- » Jumping beans: Jump!
- » Runner beans: Run on the spot.
- » Chili beans: Shiver and shake.
- » Jelly beans: Wobble and shake like jelly.
- » French beans: Do the can-can with a partner.
- » Beans in the pot: Act like any bean.

- » Coffee beans: Be very energetic.
- » String beans: Stand tall with your arms over your head.
- » Mighty beans: Either do push-ups or flex your biceps.
- » Navy beans: Stand at attention and salute.
- » Bean there: Take two steps back. Say, "Bean there," as you take two steps forward.
- » Has bean: Lie on the floor in a heap.

» **INSTRUCTIONS**

The group acts out the bean shapes as the leader calls them out.

» **SUGGESTED MUSIC**

Use the get-moving songs from the *Everybody Move!* CD.

» **VARIATIONS**

- » Have players join in small groups and call out types of beans to each other, taking turns.
- » Have players teach some of these actions to someone they meet that day (family member, friend).

Safety Tip

Ensure that players have enough room to move and will not bump into furniture or each other.

Adapted, by permission, from Ontario HPE Curriculum Support, Ophea.

» OBJECTIVE

To successfully use as many different types of throws and catches within a certain time limit

» PLAYERS

Any size group (players work on their own)

» EQUIPMENT

One piece of scrap paper per player or Hacky Sacks, tennis balls, or any other small balls. You could also create a large, light ball using two or three lightly crumpled sheets of newspaper taped together with masking tape. A plastic grocery bag can be wrapped around the ball of newspapers and taped for increased durability. These trashballs are great for other activities as well, such as sepak takraw (an Asian kick-volleyball sport), ball tag, and dodgeball (see Variations).

» SETUP

Players are in a scattered formation with enough distance between them so they will not accidentally crash into each other.

» INSTRUCTIONS

1. Players continuously throw and catch a piece of crumpled paper, trying different tricks.
2. Tricks include over the shoulder, under the leg, behind the back, and stand to toss and sit to catch.

Safety Tip
Be sure players are aware of any objects, such as desks and chairs, that might be in the way if a toss goes astray.

» VARIATIONS

» This can be done with one ball and two players or a larger group with one ball per group or one ball per player.

» Nonelimination Trash Ball: Players each make their own ball from scrap newspaper and throw it at other players below the waist. Once hit, a player must do 15 repetitions of a fitness activity such as jumping jacks before rejoining the game. The objective is to not get hit and to move continuously for the duration of the game.

» Everybody's It Ball Tag: Using lightweight trash balls, try to throw the ball at another player's legs. When hit, the tagged player sits down (and throws away any ball she may be holding) and waits until another player throws a ball to her. Then she re-enters the game.

» Pop-Up Trashball: There are no teams, and everyone starts with a trash ball. If a player gets hit below the waist, he must sit on the spot where he was hit while the game continues. He may rejoin the game when the person who hit him gets hit. (When the person who hit a lot of people gets hit, a huge number of people suddenly pop up and rejoin the game.)

>> **OBJECTIVE**

For players to individually enact the movements of the story

>> **PLAYERS**

Any number

>> **EQUIPMENT**

None required

>> **SETUP**

Players are in a scattered formation around the room.

>> **INSTRUCTIONS**

1. Players move around the room, acting out different animals. For example, a lumbering bear, a hopping bunny, a jumping frog, a slithering snake, a waddling penguin or seal, a galloping horse, a flying or hopping bird, a walking chicken, a rumbling elephant, a chopping crocodile. . . . Ask the players for more ideas!
2. Animals can move with or without sound.

>> **VARIATION**

Use the following story with players in kindergarten or a primary grade.

Active Animal Story

Read each bold word to your players, and have them mimic it. Then read the following story and have the players act it out. Allow a pause after each bold word in order for players to have the opportunity to move like that animal for a few seconds.

On a rainy day, the players went on a water trip in their **rowboat** with their **lame dog**. It barked all day because a **crab was pinching its tail**. **Lightning struck a tree**, and **a log hit the boat**. The **players ran** for cover ashore, but a bear blocked the way to the woods. It didn't help that a **slimy snake slithered** in the grass nearby. Even the **frogs had to jump** for cover. Suddenly a **kangaroo hopped** to the rescue but stopped short when an **alligator crawled** into sight. It was only **sunning itself**, but soon a **cat chased a mouse** across the path. This frightened a **rabbit**, and it **hopped quickly** behind a bush. The gate to the zoo was nearby, and statues of eagles guarded it, but the **players ran** past them into the penguin house and saw the **seals as they slid off** the ice and into the cold water. The donkeys were around the corner next to the cage for the gorillas, but when the **inchworm crossed** the path of the frightened players, they decided to **gallop like the horses** and **leap like the antelope** back to the bus for safety. They **sat down quietly** on the bus. The rainy day was full of adventure!

» OBJECTIVE

For players to create their own activity cards and then to be active with them as they are selected

» PLAYERS

Any number

» EQUIPMENT

» Index cards
» Pens or pencils

» SETUP

1. Each player chooses a fitness activity that can be done in place, gives it a name, and writes it on an index card or scrap paper with a simple illustration.
2. Each player demonstrates his activity for the group.
3. Place all the cards in front of the room.
4. Two players are in front of the room.

» INSTRUCTIONS

Two players are up front: One leads the class for 30 seconds, the other player studies her card and leads for the next 30 seconds. When the first player returns to his place, the next player picks up a card and prepares to lead the next 30 seconds of activity.

» SUGGESTED MUSIC

Use energizing music to keep the players moving. Use the *Everybody Move!* CD 30-second music clips.

Safety Tip
Ensure players stay in their own space while moving around.

» VARIATIONS

» Circle the Room: Players leave their own activity cards on their own desks. After 30 seconds, players move around the room and stand beside another desk for the next 30 seconds of activity.
» Group Activity: Players work in groups and create an activity and station cards for that activity. Groups rotate together from one activity to the next.

FITNESS ROLL

» OBJECTIVE

For each player to complete the following activities designated by numbers on dice.

» PLAYERS

Any number

» EQUIPMENT

- » List of activities that correspond to the numbers on the dice
- » 15 to 20 pairs of dice

» SETUP

1. Divide players into groups of two.
2. Give each group two dice.
3. Designate a safe area within the activity area for each group.

» INSTRUCTIONS

1. Each player rolls one die. The player who rolls the highest number jogs around the outside of the activity area two times. If the two players roll the same number, they must both roll again.

2. The player who rolls the lowest number rolls both dice two times—once to determine the corresponding activity designated by the total of the two dice, and the second time to indicate how many times to perform the exercise.

3. Activities may include the following:

   Roll of 2: marching on the spot

   Roll of 3: sit-ups

   Roll of 4: wall push-ups

   Roll of 5: tuck jumps

   Roll of 6: line jumps

   Roll of 7: lunges

   Roll of 8: chicken jacks

   Roll of 9: jogging on the spot

   Roll of 10: wall jumps

   Roll of 11: floor push-ups

   Roll of 12: mountain climbers

Adapted, by permission, from Ontario Education, 2005, *Healthy schools: Daily physical activity in schools- grades 7 and 8* (Ontario: Ontario Education).

ATHLETIC MOVES

» OBJECTIVE

Players mimic sport moves

» PLAYERS

Any number

» EQUIPMENT

None required

» SETUP

Players are in a scattered formation around the room.

» INSTRUCTIONS

1. Players move around the room like athletes from different sports (e.g., basketball, hockey, football).
2. The leader calls out, "Freeze!" approximately every 30 seconds.
3. Players freeze in a shape to show their sport.
4. Have players guess what sports two others are representing.
5. Each time players begin to move again, challenge them to move like a different athlete from a different sport.

» SUGGESTED MUSIC

Use energetic music from the *Everybody Move!* CD. Pause music for players to freeze. "Elementary Circuit" selections would allow movement for 30 seconds and a pause between each song.

SPEED-WALK SHUFFLE

» OBJECTIVE

For each group to get as many objects as possible within the time limit

» PLAYERS

Any number

» EQUIPMENT

30 to 40 marbles (or trashballs, beanbags, math manipulatives, popsicle sticks . . .)

» SETUP

1. This is a relay activity. Divide players into teams of three.
2. Divide teams so that half are on one side of the room and half are on the other side.
3. All groups have a pile of marbles, the same number on each side.

» INSTRUCTIONS

1. Play music. Players move (jog, jump, dance) in place to the music.
2. On the signal to begin, the first person in each line (on both sides of the room) picks up a marble, speed-walks down her aisle to the other side of the room (players pass each other on the right), places the marble in the pile on the opposite side, then speed-walks back. As soon as the first person is back, the second person starts the same action.
3. While one person is speed-walking, have the waiting line do activities that raise the heart rate. For example, jumping jacks, gluteal kicks, or jogging on the spot.
4. Challenge teams to make the pile on the opposite side larger than their own by moving quickly.

» SUGGESTED MUSIC

Use lively music like song 16 "Rock Shot" or song 17 "Rock and Roll."

Safety Tip

To control speed, have players move with their feet on small carpet pieces (easily picked up as scraps from a carpet store) or have players walk heel to toe, with the toe of one foot bumping into the heel of the other.

» VARIATIONS

When playing in a gymnasium or outside, players can run, skip, or hop instead of speed walking.

SPEED SIMON SAYS

>> **OBJECTIVE**

To only do activities that the leader begins with "Simon says"

>> **PLAYERS**

Any number

>> **EQUIPMENT**

None required

>> **SETUP**

1. Set up two games of Simon Says, one at the front of the room and one at the back.
2. A leader faces each group.

>> **INSTRUCTIONS**

1. The leader speaks as quickly as possible and makes instructions as aerobic as possible (move large muscles, do big movements). If players move when the leader does not preface the instructions with "Simon Says," they move into the other Simon Says game. If they make a mistake there, they move back to the first game. Challenge players to switch games as little as possible.

2. Ideas for aerobic instructions include run on the spot, jump up and down with two feet, hop on one foot, or do big arm circles. See Funky Moves (starting on page 122) or the list of activities used for Fitness Spelling (page 54) for other activity ideas.

»» *SUGGESTED MUSIC*

Song 20 ("Mission Improbable") from the *Everybody Move!* CD.

🔅 *Safety Tip*
Ensure players stay in their own space while doing movements.

»» *VARIATIONS*

» One-Leader Speed Simon Says: All players begin on one side of the room. Only one leader does all the calling. When players make an error, they quickly go to the other half of the room and continue to follow the leader. If they make another error, they move back to the original side. The players who switch sides the fewest times are the winners.

» Four-Corner Speed Simon Says: A leader is in each corner of the room. Divide the players into the corners to follow the leaders. When players make an error, they move clockwise to the next leader. Winners are the ones who move the fewest spots.

HEALTHY SIMON SAYS

» OBJECTIVE

For players to complete the activities when "Simon says," using their knowledge of healthy living strategies

» PLAYERS

Any number (the teacher can be Simon, or a player can be chosen to lead the group)

» EQUIPMENT

A list of health and active living questions

» SETUP

1. Choose one person to stand at the front of the group and be Simon.
2. Have participants spread out around the play area.

» INSTRUCTIONS

1. The leader calls out an action by saying, "Simon says . . ." followed by a healthy statement and an action.
2. If the statement is true, players move accordingly.
3. If the statement is false, the players continue doing the action they are currently doing.
4. If a player changes his action after a false statement, discuss why the statement is false, and then continue with the game.

Examples: As an exit assignment at the end of a day, class, or unit, have each student prepare three cards each with a true or false question related to the unit you are studying. Use these cards for the Healthy Simon Says game.

Fitness examples:

If stretching is a stress management technique, reach for your toes. (True)

If being active every day will improve your fitness level, jog on the spot. (True)

If push-ups are a strength activity, do 10 push-ups. (True)

If going for a five-minute walk does wonders for your heart, do five jumping jacks. (False)

Math examples:

If 5 times 5 equals 25, do five jumping jacks. (True)

If 15 divided by 3 equals 4, run one lap of the room. (False)

If 2 times 15 equals 30, do 10 mountain climbers. (True)

Nutrition examples:

If eating lots of saturated fat is helpful for you because it gives you lots of energy, do 10 sit-ups. (False)

If eating oranges is a great source of vitamin D, do a sideways stretch on either side. (False)

If drinking milk is a great source of vitamin D and calcium, stretch your arms behind your back at shoulder level. (True)

» VARIATIONS

» Run Both Ways: Line up four pylons that players run around in a clockwise direction. When the answer is *false*, they turn around and run in a counterclockwise direction. If the answer is true, they continue to run the same way. Stress the importance of observing personal space so students avoid colliding when changing directions or while running in opposite directions.

» That's Me: Players begin by sitting at their desks. Read a statement. If the answer is *true*, students stand up quickly (and safely), call out "that's me!," and sit down again. Read the next statement. This can be a great activity at the beginning of the year to quickly help you get to know your students better. Following are some sample questions.

That's Me statements:

I have blue eyes.

I have a younger brother.

I have an older sister.

I am the oldest child in my family.

I am the youngest child in my family.

I have brown eyes.

I can touch my nose with the tip of my tongue.

I can curl my tongue.

I have moved more than two times in my life.

I walk to school most days.

I love milk.

I usually have cereal for breakfast.

I eat at least one fruit a day.

My favorite sport is soccer.

My favorite sport is baseball.

I play an instrument.

I can whistle.

I have seen the ocean.

I have a grandparent who lives in the same city as I do.

My favorite subject in school is art.

I finished reading a book during the last two weeks.

I read a part of a newspaper during this past week.

I slept more than eight hours last night.

I think I will travel to the moon during my life.

I went to a church, temple, or mosque during the last week.

MAGNETIC FORCE FIELD

» OBJECTIVE

For players to "repel" each other as they walk around the room

» PLAYERS

Any number

» EQUIPMENT

None required

» SETUP

1. Players are in a scattered formation around the room.
2. This activity is useful for developing awareness of the playing space.

» INSTRUCTIONS

1. Players speed-walk around the classroom. Challenge players to move as if they had a two-foot (half-meter) force field around themselves so that they cannot touch anyone or anything else. Their force field causes them to repel off other objects and people (without touching) and change direction.
2. Change the form of locomotion so players are walking, hopping, skipping, jumping, or galloping around the space.
3. If there are too many players, have players line up in groups of three or four. When the front of the magnet hits another group's force field, the whole line turns around and goes the other way. Start slowly, but atoms pick up speed when they get warm, so the players can move more quickly as their bodies warm up.

○ Safety Tip

To control speed, have players move with their feet on small carpet pieces (easily picked up as scraps from a carpet store), or have players walk heel to toe, with the toe of one foot bumping into the heel of the other.

» VARIATION

Repelling and Attracting Magnets: When players meet face to face, they repel each other; when they catch up behind someone, they attract and put their hands on the front player's shoulders. When the magnet is repelled, everyone in the magnet turns around so the front person is now on the back and the back person is now on the front. Eventually there will be one long line of players, and you are ready to take the students to the library, lunch room, or other place you needed them to line up for.

PRACTICE TAG

» OBJECTIVE

To not get tagged by the tagger

» PLAYERS

Any number

» EQUIPMENT

None required, although a pool noodle for each "it" is safer and more fun

» SETUP

Select one tagger ("it") for every 10 players. This ratio depends on the grade level and ability of the class as well as the comfort of the leader.

» INSTRUCTIONS

1. Players play tag by speed-walking around the classroom. When caught, they do an identified activity (e.g., skip around the classroom, complete a hopscotch course, throw and catch a ball five times, or anything else they might be working on in physical education) and then return to the game.

2. Give the players a chance to choose the activity they need to perform before returning to the game. If possible, align the activity with a skill they are learning in their physical education class to give them an opportunity to practice.

Safety Tip

Make sure the tagged players perform the identified activity safely out of bounds of the tag game.

TAG !!

JUMP THE ANSWER

» OBJECTIVE

For players to jump the answers to math questions

» PLAYERS

Any number

» EQUIPMENT

None required

» SETUP

A leader faces players who are standing.

» INSTRUCTIONS

Read math questions appropriate to the level of the players. Players listen to the question and "jump the answer" by jumping a certain number of times. For example, for 20 minus 5, the players would jump 15 times.

» VARIATIONS

» Vary the kinds of jumps: tuck jumps with knees up, forward and backward, side to side, stride with one foot forward and one back.

» Group Question and Answer: One group jumps the question (jump 5 times, say *plus*, and then jump 6 more times), and the other group responds (11 jumps).

12- 13 - 14 - 15

GRAB BAG IMPROVISATION

» OBJECTIVE

Moving around according to the object selected

» PLAYERS

Any number

» EQUIPMENT

Bag filled with various objects: toy vehicles, plastic animals, egg beaters, tops, or springs

» SETUP

1. Players are in a scattered formation around the room.
2. The leader has a bag filled with various objects (could be varied or around a theme, such as jungle animals or industrial vehicles).

» INSTRUCTIONS

1. Pull one object out of the bag at a time. Players look at the object and then move their bodies in a way that corresponds with the object.
2. Encourage players to make their actions big so that their hearts beat fast. For example, if the object is a truck, the students pretend to steer a big wheel while walking quickly.

» SUGGESTED MUSIC

Pick appropriate music. For example, if you are picking from barnyard animals, repeating song 26 "Crazy Farm" and song 27 "Chicken Ribs" on the *Everybody Move!* CD is fun.

» VARIATION

Have players bring objects from home to place in the bag.

Adapted, by permission, from Ontario HPE Curriculum Support, Ophea.

SCARF PATTERNS

» OBJECTIVE

For players to make patterns with scarves

» PLAYERS

Any number

» EQUIPMENT

- » 1 scarf per player
- » Index cards and pens or pencils
- » Chalk and board

» SETUP

Players are in a scattered formation around the room, each holding a scarf.

» INSTRUCTIONS

1. Create a series of patterns on the board or on index cards. Working with one pattern at a time, players use a scarf (necktie, ribbon, crepe paper, tissue) to trace the pattern in the air.
2. Players can create their own pattern cards and contribute to a class set.
3. Encourage players to use big movements and to make patterns as large as possible.

» SUGGESTED MUSIC

Play some flowing music, such as song 37 "Shammusa" from the *Everybody Move!* CD.

» VARIATIONS

- » Players sit in chairs and follow patterns by waving their hands or feet in the air.
- » Have players "write" their names or spelling words in the air.
- » Juggling: Have players learn to juggle using three light scarves.

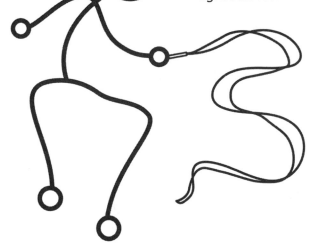

BYE-BYE

» OBJECTIVE

To not get tagged by the "it"

» PLAYERS

Groups of 5 to 30

» EQUIPMENT

Desks or hula hoops

» SETUP

1. Identify one player (or more) to be "it."
2. Create two or three safe zones. Safe zones can be desks or hula hoops in an open space.

» INSTRUCTIONS

1. On the signal to begin, players who are "it" chase the others.
2. Players move by speed-walking if playing in a classroom.
3. If tagged, players do a designated activity and then return to the game.
4. Players are safe from being caught if they are touching a designated safe area.
5. If one player is in the safe area and another comes up and says, "Bye-bye," the first player must immediately leave the safe area. Only one can be there at a time. Players cannot bump the person out of the safe area who bumped them (i.e., no "bump backs").

Safety Tip

Communicate to players before playing the game the importance of no body contact and no pushing.

» VARIATIONS

» If players are not active enough, add more "its."
» To control speed, have players move with their feet on small carpet pieces (easily picked up as scraps from a carpet store), or have players walk heel to toe, with the toe of one foot bumping into the heel of the other.

MATH MATCH

» OBJECTIVE

To match up questions with answers

» PLAYERS

Any number

» EQUIPMENT

Question and answer cards

» SETUP

1. Make math question and answer cards, with each question card having a matching answer card.

2. Place these cards facedown on the desks or the floor to begin.

» INSTRUCTIONS

1. Players move around the room (hopping, jogging, and skipping).

2. On the signal to begin, they pick up a card and try to find the person with the matching card. For example, a player with a card reading "5 × 7" finds the person with a card reading "35."

3. When a player finds his match, he does a fitness task with his partner (e.g., five bench step-ups), returns his cards to the leader, and continues to move around the room.

4. When everyone is finished, the leader can mix up the cards and redistribute them at random or have the players put them facedown on the desk at which they completed the activity.

» VARIATIONS

» Verbs and Adverbs: Create cards with verbs and adverbs (one per card). Have players find a match and then act out what the combination says (e.g., "dance" "quickly," "jump" "elegantly," "walk" "smoothly."

» Create cards that reinforce other concepts (e.g., capitals with states, provinces, or countries; food groups; history dates and events). Have students develop two cards each as an exit activity for a unit, class, or day.

Adapted, by permission, from Ontario HPE Curriculum Support, Ophea.

0	0 ÷ 1
1	1 ÷ 1
2	2 ÷ 1
3	3 ÷ 1
4	4 ÷ 1
5	5 ÷ 1
6	
7	
8	
9	
10	
11	
12	

Verb	Adverb
dance	quickly
walk	elegantly
	slowly
	secretly
	lightly
	heavily
	...tically
	...sically
	...gerly
	...onally
	...ously
	...pily
	...ously
	...ully

Locomotor action	Pathway/Shape/Speed
walk	curvy
run	zigzag
jump	straight
gallop	curled
hop	twisted
skip	sideways
leap	heavy
crawl	light
slither	slow
swivel	fast
wiggle	low
glide	high
spin	stretched
slide	wide
march	narrow
contract	diagonally
expand	backward
bend	forward

WHO'S COMING?

>> **OBJECTIVE**

To walk and then follow instructions when "someone is coming"

>> **PLAYERS**

Any number

>> **EQUIPMENT**

None required

>> **SETUP**

Players are in a scattered formation around the room.

>> **INSTRUCTIONS**

1. Teach the group actions that correspond with school events and activities (see examples provided). You may want to post the list on the blackboard or an overhead.
2. Throughout the challenge, the group does the activities as the leader calls them out.

Suggested actions for Who's Coming?:

Principal's coming: Sit in your chair with your hands folded, keeping your feet marching.

Recess: Jump up and run on the spot.

Teacher's coming: Sit in your chair with your feet marching and one hand stretched in the air.

Forgot homework: Stand up and run in a circle (around your desk or in place).

Field trip: Sit in your chair and bounce up and down on your seat to mimic a bus ride.

>> **SUGGESTED MUSIC**

Fast-paced music from the *Everybody Move!* CD, such as song 6 "Latinique" or song 21 "Stadium Rock," or from other CDs, such as "Be True to Your School" by the Beach Boys.

>> **VARIATIONS**

» Players can remain seated in chairs, marching feet and swinging arms, in place of marching around the classroom.

» Move to other themes such as visiting Texas, where players gallop around the room and then respond to statements like "Lasso the cow"—hopping on one spot and pretending to get ready to lasso a cow; "Dallas Cowboys are coming"—players repeatedly pretend to throw and catch a football; or "Texas Rangers hit a home run"—players repeatedly run in a small circle.

Adapted, by permission, from ACTIV8, Ophea.

»» OBJECTIVE

For players to move as they spell different words (a great activity for practicing spelling)

»» PLAYERS

Any number

»» EQUIPMENT

Poster board of the ABCs of fitness, or activity cards posted around the room.

»» SETUP

1. On a poster board, list the alphabet provided and the corresponding activity.
2. The leader is by the poster board, and the players are in a scattered formation facing the poster board.

»» INSTRUCTIONS

Players follow the leader through the ABCs of fitness:

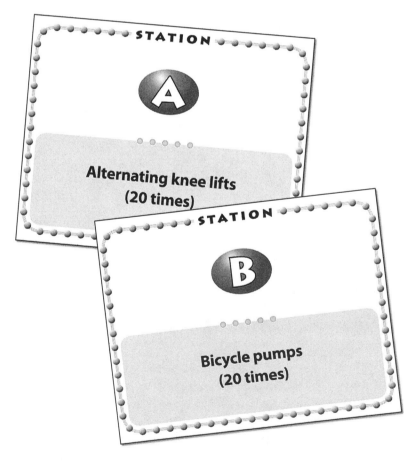

A: alternating knee lifts (20 times)

B: bicycle pumps (20 times)

C: calf lifts (20 times)

D: dips (10 times)

E: Energizer Bunny hops (20 times)

F: funky fish (8 times)

G: gluteal kicks (10 times each leg)

H: hop on each foot (10 times)

I: intense march on spot (20 seconds)

J: jumping jacks (20 times)

K: kicks to front, side, and back (10 times each)

L: lunges on each leg (10 times)

M: mountain climbers (15 times)

N: Nordic skiing (20 times)

O: overhead serve (10 times)

P: push-ups (5 times)

Q: quick ski jumps, side to side (10 times)

R: run on the spot (15 seconds)

S: skip on the spot, knees high (20 seconds)

T: tuck jumps (5 times)

U: up and down (5 times)

V: V sit (20 seconds)

W: walk and clap (4 times)

X: XL (extra large) arm circles
(10 times in each direction)

Y: yardwork—rake leaves (10 times each side)

Z: zigzag jumps, side to side
(20 times)

Note: Each letter of the alphabet corresponds with the first letter of each activity to help with memory. However, substitutions can be made to accommodate all players.

» VARIATIONS

» Have players spell their own name.

» Have players work in pairs (one spells a word by doing the actions for each letter; the other partner guesses the word).

» Skipping and Tripping: Players jump rope and recite the alphabet as they jump. When they trip, they do the activity for the letter they tripped on and then start at A again. Students who can successfully skip through the entire alphabet keep skipping after Z, beginning again with A. Excellent rope jumpers can challenge themselves with more difficult moves such as "double unders," where the rope passes two times under their feet with each jump.

» Place alphabet letter cards (or foam letters) around the room with a copy of the Fitness Spelling activities, and play music. Have players move in pairs and do the activities for the letter on the card. Stop the music every 20 to 30 seconds, and have players move to the next letter.

» Elimination Return: Place the alphabet letter cards facedown. In any game in which a player is eliminated, she goes to the cards, selects one, does the activity on the card, and returns to the game again.

AMAZING RACE

» **OBJECTIVE**

For players to complete the instructions at each station

» **PLAYERS**

Any number

» **EQUIPMENT**

- » Four pylons
- » Four skipping ropes
- » 20 tennis balls, one small pail
- » Four beanbags
- » Four pool noodles

» **SETUP**

Set up stations around the classroom, and distribute the players evenly at each station.

» **INSTRUCTIONS**

Students rotate around the centers with a partner, spending one minute at each center or region.

» **SUGGESTED MUSIC**

Use the 30-second music pieces on the *Everybody Move!* CD.

STATION

1

AUSTRALIA

Do kangaroo hops around the pylons

STATION

2

CANADA

Take a bobsled run around the room, each partner holding the end of a skipping rope.

Station	Activity
Station 1: Australia	Kangaroo hops around the pylons.
Station 2: Canada	Take a bobsled run around the room, each partner holding the end of a skipping rope.
Station 3: Jamaica/Caribbean	Coconut shuttle. Deposit balls using the knees. Place a ball between the knees, hop to the pail and drop the ball in, and run back. Repeat until signal.
Station 4: United States	Climb the mountains: While in full layout push-up position, alternate your legs as you bring them to your chest as if you are climbing stairs.
Station 5: Russia	In the crab-walk position, kick your legs out one at a time (advanced level: cross arms in front, and kick feet out while squatting).
Station 6: Japan	Sushi roll: Roll across a designated area. Keep the sushi roll tight!
Station 7: Egypt	Do Egyptian walks or lunges across the room.
Station 8: France	Compete in the Tour de France by bicycling on your back (get hips off ground).
Station 9: Mexico	Hot tamale beanbag toss between partners. Keep track of the number of completed tosses without dropping the beanbag.
Station 10: Greece	Run the Olympic torch (pool noodle) through the countries.

» *VARIATION*

Elimination Hoops: Place the station cards on the wall around the gym or large space. Place one hula hoop per person in a circle in the middle of the gym. Remove one hoop. Players stand around the circle of hoops. As the music plays, players move in a specified locomotion pattern (i.e., walking, jogging, skipping, galloping, hopping on one foot, etc.) clockwise around the hoops. When the music stops, players must stand inside a hoop. If two players go into the same hoop, the first player in the hoop can stay. If it is a tie, one can choose to leave or they play a quick game of rock, paper, scissors, with the winner staying in the hoop. The one person (or more if you eliminate more hoops each time) goes to the first station and performs the prescribed exercise when the music is going. Remove another hoop or hoops, and start the music again. Stop the music, and once more another player or players are eliminated. The players who were at station 1 now go to station 2, and the players who were just eliminated go to station 1. Continue until only one person is left. Play again.

CLIMBERS AND SLIDERS

» OBJECTIVE

To be the first to land or go past 100 and sing the chorus of "We Are the Champions"

» PLAYERS

Any number

» EQUIPMENT

- » One Climbers and Sliders board per group (printed out from the DVD-ROM and laminated on a poster board) and one die and one marker per board; for kindergarten and grade primary players, use the Climbers and Sliders Activity Board for Primary Players if they cannot read well enough yet to read the instructions on the One Hundred Activities Chart for Primary Players

- » 100 Activities Chart (use the 100 Activities Chart for Primary Players as necessary)

- » Have players imagine when equipment is suggested (or provide it: skipping ropes, basketballs, hula hoops, and so on)

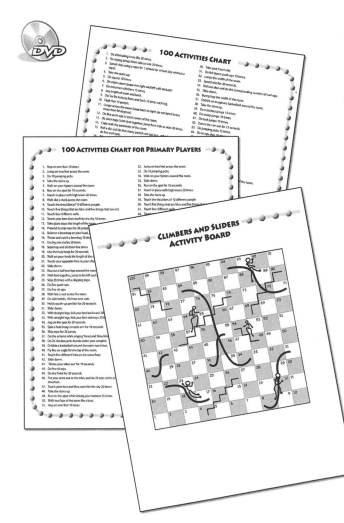

» SETUP

Assign players to groups, and give each group a board, die, and marker.

» INSTRUCTIONS

1. Groups start with their markers off the board.

2. One player throws the die and moves the marker forward the required number of spaces—if the marker lands on a stairs, the marker moves to the top of the stairs; if it lands on a slide, the marker moves to the bottom of the slide.

3. Wherever the marker ends, the group completes the activity for that spot and then throws and moves again.

Note: Some of these activities can be found in the Funky Moves descriptions starting on page 122.

»» *VARIATIONS*

- » Individual Climbers and Sliders: Several students each play their own game on the board. Players decide who will go first. Player 1 rolls the die, moves her marker to the designated space on the game board, then proceeds to do the activity that corresponds with the number (e.g., space 14—crab-walk the perimeter of the room). While player 1 is doing her activity, player 2 rolls the die and proceeds to do the corresponding activity for his roll.

- » A second game board includes pictures of animals on top of each column. For younger children, instruct them to move around the room or gym like the animal pictured at the top of the column on which they landed.

Safety Tips

- ✻ *Make sure players are using the proper techniques while completing the tasks.*
- ✻ *Have players complete a full-body stretch to cool down after the activity.*

CLASSROOM TRIATHLON

» **OBJECTIVE**

For players to complete a triathlon

» **PLAYERS**

Any number

» **EQUIPMENT**

Chairs to sit on (optional)

» **SETUP**

Players are in a scattered formation around the room sitting in their chairs.

» **INSTRUCTIONS**

The leader calls out different events while players do actions.

Swimming: Do large arm strokes such as front crawl, butterfly, and breaststroke.

Cycling: Lean back in chair with legs in air, and pedal with legs.

Running: Move legs in air as if running a race.

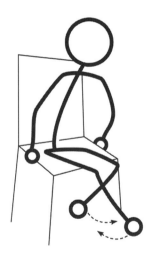 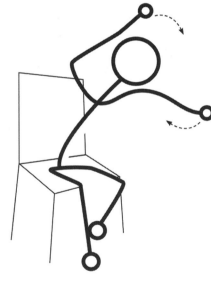 

Safety Tip

Remind players to make sure all four legs of the chair are on the ground at all times.

» **VARIATION**

Have players design their own fun and wacky triathlons to include such activities as dancing, climbing, crawling, skiing, skating, or scuba diving.

BALLOON KEEP-UP

OBJECTIVE

For each team to keep a balloon in the air with as many consecutive hits as possible

PLAYERS

Small groups around a table, students in four to six desks facing each other, or groups of four to six seated in chairs in a tight circle

EQUIPMENT

One balloon per group

SETUP

1. Each player is seated in a tight circle of players.
2. One person is given a balloon.

INSTRUCTIONS

1. When the players are ready, the player with the balloon hits it into the air so another player can hit it. Players cannot hit the balloon twice in a row.
2. The group counts aloud the number of consecutive hits they make before the balloon goes astray and can't be hit into the air (the students must stay in their chairs).

Safety Tip

Be sure no one in the group has a latex allergy.

VARIATION

» Instead of counting in ones, count in multiples of two, three, four. . . .
» Instead of counting, younger students can also practice going through the alphabet (forward and backward).
» If the activity is too easy, use two or more balloons per group.

CLASSROOM FOOSBALL

» OBJECTIVE

For each team to score as many points as possible against the opposing team

» PLAYERS

Works best with a smaller number of players but is suitable for a regular class of 20 to 30

» EQUIPMENT

- » Masking tape
- » One chair per player
- » Gator Skin ball or Nerf soccer ball
- » Four pylons

» SETUP

1. Desks should be pushed to the side so they are not in the way.
2. Divide the players into two teams.
3. Divide the room in half by placing masking tape on the floor.
4. Each team receives two pylons to use as their net. Nets should be placed on either end of the classroom.
5. Chairs are organized on each side of the classroom like a foosball table.
6. Each player should be sitting on a chair on his team's side of the classroom.

» INSTRUCTIONS

1. Teams do rock, paper, scissors or flip a coin for first serve.
2. Players must stay seated in their chairs at all times during the game and use the sides of their feet to kick the ball.
3. A point is scored when the ball hits the wall between the opposing team's pylons.

» VARIATIONS

- » Use two or more balls to increase the amount of physical activity.
- » Use a smaller ball.

PINBALL

» OBJECTIVE

For players to kick a ball between the chairs of other players

» PLAYERS

Groups of 6 to 10

» EQUIPMENT

- » One chair per player
- » Gator Skin ball or Nerf soccer ball

» SETUP

Players are seated in a circle facing inward, with chairs one to two yards or meters apart.

» INSTRUCTIONS

1. Players try to kick the ball (with the sides of their feet) between the chairs of two other players—when successful, the kicking player scores a point.
2. Play again for a set time limit.
3. The player with the most goals wins.

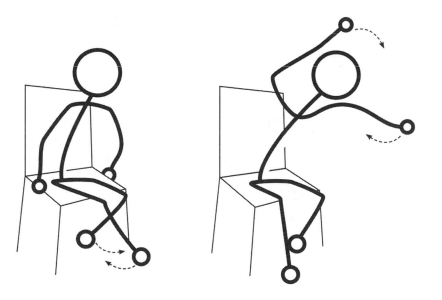

SPELLING RELAY

» **OBJECTIVE**

To be the first team to spell a selected vocabulary word

» **PLAYERS**

Any number

» **EQUIPMENT**

200 Popsicle sticks

» **SETUP**

1. Divide the players into equal teams.
2. Assign each team an equal number of Popsicle sticks, which are placed on a table across the room.

» **INSTRUCTIONS**

1. Call out a vocabulary word for teams to spell.
2. On the signal to begin, the first players on each team run to their piles, grab a stick, and bring it back to their team.
3. Upon returning, the runners tag the next player and they run and collect another stick. Meanwhile, teammates work together to spell out the vocabulary word with the sticks. Players are not allowed to break the sticks.
4. The first team to spell the word correctly wins.

» **VARIATIONS**

» To shorten this activity, players could bring back two or more sticks at a time.
» Have players define the vocabulary term after spelling it correctly.
» This activity could also be used in math. Use equations instead of vocabulary words, and have players form the correct answer with the sticks.

Based on Alberta Education, *Daily physical activity: A handbook for grades 1-9 schools* (Edmonton, AB: Alberta Education, 2006), p. 54.

CHAIR AEROBICS

OBJECTIVE

For players to follow the leader's instructions and do the activities

PLAYERS

Any number

EQUIPMENT

One chair for each person

SETUP

Players sit (or stand) facing the leader.

INSTRUCTIONS

Players do the actions as demonstrated by the leader.

Warm-up exercises:

1. Blowing in the wind: Raise arms overhead, slowly waving side to side.
2. Bobble head: Tilt head to right, left, and down.
3. Shoulder rolls: Roll shoulders forward and backward.
4. "I don't know": Do shoulder shrugs.
5. Pick apples: Reach right arm overhead to left and left arm overhead to right.
6. Monkeys: Alternately move arms up and down in front of body.
7. Double-Dutch ankles: Make alternating circles with ankles.
8. Double-Dutch wrists: Make alternating circles with wrists.
9. Dog paddle: Make small forward circles with hands.
10. Hot seat: Shift side to side in chair.
11. Dig it: Dig heels into the floor, pushing arms forward.
12. Swim it: Do breaststroke, front crawl, backstroke, butterfly, and sidestroke.
13. Macho man: Do biceps curls to each side.
14. Wave: With palm facing down, forearm parallel to floor, make wave actions across body.
15. Soldier march: March with high knees and marching arms.
16. Disco: Point right arm diagonally up (finger pointed) to the right, then down across left hip; repeat other side.
17. Step on the bug: Do toe touches to each side.
18. Kick it!: Alternately kick right and left legs to front.
19. Look out: With right hand shading eyes, look to the right; with left hand shading eyes, look to the left.
20. It's me!: Stand up and sit down.

Heart rate raisers and muscle-strengthening exercises (sitting):

1. V step: March out-out, in-in; hands go out-out, in-in.
2. Going places: With hands in front, rapidly touch right knee to right hand and left knee to left hand.

(continued)

Chair Aerobics *(continued)*

3. Soccer dribble: Dribble imaginary soccer ball with feet.

4. Tuck lifts: Lift both knees to chest.

5. Tour de bicycle: Lean back on seat and ride bicycle.

6. Shadow boxing: Circle hands over each other at head height to left; repeat to right, front, and back.

7. Cross-country skiing: Big arm swings forward and back and alternately shuffle feet forward and back.

8. Raise the roof: With palms facing toward roof, push arms up, two times to left and two times to right.

9. Flutter board kicks: Alternately lift legs up and down.

10. Clapping square: Clap hands high (once each) to right and left, then clap low right and left.

11. Flood!: Raise legs off floor and hold for 10 seconds.

12. Basketball dribble: Dribble imaginary basketball from side to side.

13. Oops!: Stand and lower buttocks to just above seat height.

14. Speedskater: Extend right leg to right side and arms to left; extend left leg to left side and arms to right.

15. Cross crawl: Lift right knee to left elbow and left knee to right elbow.

16. Bottoms up: Push down on chair and raise buttocks off chair.

17. Give me space: With arms bent at elbow, chest height, push hands out to side and back.

18. Jump it: Jump imaginary rope while sitting.

19. Just do it!: Swim, cycle, and jog.

20. Chicken jacks: While sitting, lift elbows up and down.

Heart rate raisers and muscle-strengthening exercises (standing):

1. Cross crawl: Bring opposite hand to opposite knee.

2. Lunges: Stand beside chair and lunge forward, alternating legs.

3. Back leg lifts: Stand behind chair, lift each leg back as high as possible, and hold.

4. Side leg lifts: Stand with your side to back of chair and lift leg to side; repeat other leg.

5. Front leg lifts: Stand beside chair and lift leg high to front; repeat other leg.

6. Seat taps: Stand facing seat, and alternately lift legs and touch front of seat.

7. Hamstring curls: Stand behind chair, and alternately lift heels toward buttocks.

8. Skip to my Lou: Skip in place, turning an imaginary rope.

9. Walk it/march it: Walk or march around chair.

10. Jumping jacks: Jump legs into straddle position, arms raised to V shape above head; jump legs together, bringing arms to side. Repeat.

Cool-Down Exercises

1. Did you see that?: Look around from side to side.
2. Pick it up: Bend to right then left side, pretending to pick something up.
3. Leg circles: Make large circles with each leg.
4. Knee hugs: Alternately hug each knee.
5. Shake your sillies out: Shake arms, fingers, and legs vigorously.
6. Shoulder rolls: Roll shoulders forward and backward.
7. Ankle circles: Make circles with ankles.
8. Wrist and elbow circles: Make circles with wrists, then circle elbows forward and backward.
9. Where are my toes?: Leaning forward, touch ankles and toes.
10. Smell the roses: Take deep breaths in (raise arms out to side and up) and breathe out (shaking hands on way down).

» SUGGESTED MUSIC

Adding music to this activity is helpful. Select an active song for most of the activities, and choose a cool-down song from the *Everybody Move!* CD for the cool-down section.

» VARIATIONS

- » Have students come up with moves.
- » Teachers or leaders can choose activities that are appropriate to the abilities of the participants. For example, a student in a wheelchair may still successfully participate in many selected activities.
- » Additional moves can be found in chapter 7.

CHAPTER 4

Activities for Spaces In and Around the Building

The games in this chapter require spaces larger than a regular classroom. Typical spaces include such areas as a cafeteria, a very large classroom, a gymnasium, and even stairwells.

Line 'Em Up requires a room full of lines on the floor—a gymnasium often works well. The stairs are a great fitness tool in Stair Step-Ups—be sure to have students hold on to the rails so no one gets injured. Other activities can be done in open spaces, such as Robin's Nest or a variety of circuits. Mission Possible can be done anywhere and is delightfully noisy and chaotic, so make sure your neighbors do not require quiet when you are playing this game. Chuck the Chicken can be done in any big space. Triangle Tag is a very vigorous activity, so be sure to change the "its" regularly.

Big spaces open themselves to many activities. For another excellent resource of creative and active games in big spaces, refer to *Chicken and Noodle Games* by John Byl et al. (2007).

MISSION POSSIBLE

» OBJECTIVE

For players to complete as much of their mission as possible in the time limit

» PLAYERS

Any number

» EQUIPMENT

- » Mission cards for every three players
- » Six skipping ropes (players can pretend if you do not have any)
- » Six hula hoops (players can pretend if you do not have any)

1. Do eight sit-ups in each corner of the room.
2. Touch six different people wearing white on the back.
3. Jog one lap of the room.
4. Do three push-ups in each corner of the room.
5. Yell, "We love fitness!" in unison three times in the center of the room.
6. Jump up and down 15 times and then yell, "Feeling good!"
7. Do 12 jumping jacks on a line.
8. Shake hands with six people who are *not* on your team.
9. Skip around the room touching each wall.
10. Touch 15 different lines on the floor of the room with your left hand.
11. Touch 20 different lines on the floor of the room with your right foot.
12. Do skier hops (with feet together, jump from side to side) over a line 20 times.
13. Hop on one foot from one end of the room to the other.
14. Link arms in a group and dance the can-can 10 times.
15. In the middle of the room, do the words and actions to "Head and Shoulders, Knees and Toes."
16. Do bicycle sit-ups 10 times.
17. Jump up and down and touch the wall as high as you can 10 times.

» SETUP

1. Divide the group into teams of three, and give each team a piece of paper with their "mission" on it. This mission is a list of activities to be done in and around the space. Use the sheet provided, or take a sample of those activities, or make your own list as it relates to a unit you are doing. For example, for desert animals or modes of transportation, have students do one lap of the classroom while making their animal's sounds and moving as their animal would.

2. Players select a starting mission (number on the card).

»» *INSTRUCTIONS*

1. On the signal to begin, teams perform the missions in order as a team.

2. When moving from mission to mission, team members stay connected to each other by holding hands, linking arms, or holding onto each other's waists.

3. At the bottom of each mission, you might want to put a disclaimer such as this: "Warning: The completion of these missions will only make you stronger and much more fit. Do not attempt the missions unless you are prepared to have fun and want to get or stay in shape."

»» *SUGGESTED MUSIC*

Song 20 ("Mission Improbable") from the *Everybody Move!* CD.

»» *VARIATION*

As an alternative, teams could divide missions so that they collectively complete the tasks.

Adapted, by permission, from Ontario HPE Curriculum Support, Ophea.

KEEP IT UP TEAM CHALLENGE

» OBJECTIVE

For teams to pick up as many scrap-paper balls as possible without letting their balloon touch the floor

» PLAYERS

Teams of four

» EQUIPMENT

- » Three pylons per team
- » One balloon per team
- » 20 scrap-paper balls per team

» SETUP

1. Have each team find a playing area and place their pylons in the area to form a triangle (about 10 steps between pylons).
2. Scatter a number of scrap paper balls (or other objects) within the team's triangle.
3. One player from each team begins with the balloon at the center of the team's triangle. The remaining three players stand at each corner of the triangle.

» INSTRUCTIONS

1. On the signal to begin, the player in the center taps the balloon in the air, bends down to pick up a ball, and switches spots with another player from one of the corners.
2. The new center player taps the balloon in the air, picks up a ball, and switches places with another player.
3. Have the teams continue picking up balls and switching players for a set amount of time.
4. The team that can pick up the most balls in the time allotted wins.

» VARIATIONS

- » After each round, have the teams move the pylons farther apart to increase the size of the triangle.
- » If the team lets the balloon hit the floor, the players must toss in their balls and start over.
- » Have the teams compete against each other and themselves to set new records.
- » Individual Keep It Up Challenge: Each player has a balloon, and 200 tennis balls are scattered around the playing area. Each player keeps a balloon up and tries to retrieve as many tennis balls as possible. If he drops a tennis ball or the balloon hits the ground, he must drop all his tennis balls and start again.

LINE 'EM UP

» OBJECTIVE

For runners not to get tagged by the British bulldogs in the playing area

» PLAYERS

Groups of 5 to 10

» EQUIPMENT

- » One pool noodle per bulldog
- » A large empty room with lots of lines on the floor—most gymnasiums are ideal

» SETUP

1. You need a playing area (about the size of a volleyball court) with lots of lines.
2. Position players as in traditional bulldog, with one bulldog for every four runners. One player (bulldog) stands in the middle of the court, and the other players (runners) stand at one end of the court.

» INSTRUCTIONS

1. When the bulldog calls out, "Bulldog!" the runners run anywhere within the court boundaries and try to cross the court without getting tagged by the bulldog's pool noodle.
2. Bulldogs may run only on the lines.
3. If a runner is tagged, that runner switches places with that bulldog.
4. Play again.

STAIR STEP-UPS

OBJECTIVE

To complete stair climbing for a set amount of time

PLAYERS

Any number that can safely be on the stairs at one time

EQUIPMENT

None required

SETUP

1. Players spread out on the stairwell.
2. The stairs are a great location for physical activity. The area is usually self-contained, and it is easy to monitor students. The following is an easy-to-use stair workout that takes approximately 15 to 20 minutes to complete and will get your students sweating. The workout can be posted on a chart at the bottom of the stairs for reference.

Warm-up

Students walk up and down the stairs two times and complete a stretch after each repetition. Here is an example:

Two repeats (up and down), quad stretch

Two repeats (up and down), hamstring stretch

Two repeats (up and down), calf stretch

Two repeats (up and down), glute stretch

Two repeats (up and down), triceps stretch

Two repeats (up and down), shoulder rolls

Have participants come up with their own stretches.

Workout A

Two repeats (up and down): one step at a time (walking)

Two repeats (up and down): one step at a time (jogging)

Two repeats (up and down): two steps at a time (walking)

Two repeats (up and down): two steps at a time (jogging)

Workout B

Two repeats (up and down): one step at a time, jumping on two feet

Two repeats (up and down): one step at a time, hopping on the right foot

Two repeats (up and down): one step at a time, hopping on the left foot

Two repeats (up and down): one step at a time, bounding (jumping higher—more explosive)

(Students always walk on the way down.)

Two-minute rest. Repeat A and B as often as participants are able to—you may need to progress slowly depending on the students' fitness levels.

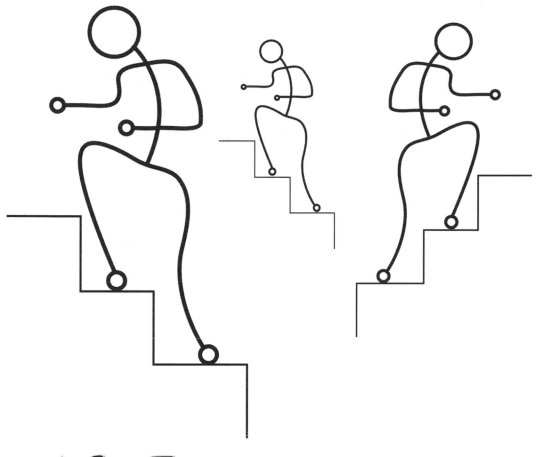

☼ *Safety Tips*

- ☀ *Students should always walk or jog up the stairs on the right-hand side with a hand either on, or close to, a railing.*
- ☀ *Students must walk down the right-hand side of the stairs—the workout portion is going up.*
- ☀ *Passing slower students should only be done on the way up.*
- ☀ *Supervise the students halfway up the stairs (on landing) if possible.*

» SUGGESTED MUSIC

Use music with a strong beat, such as song 16 "Rock Shot" from the *Everybody Move!* CD.

» VARIATIONS

» Burj Dubai Stair Climb: In this activity, students use a stairwell in the school. In short, students climb stairs to try to climb to the top of the Burj Dubai. Everyone in the class repeatedly climbs the stairs in a stairwell. Every time the last person (the caboose) gets to the landing, she is given something to record their progress (e.g., a Popsicle stick). At the end of the session, the sticks are added up, and the progress in terms of the number of floors climbed is marked on a Burj Dubai chart. The Burj Dubai has 160 floors. (You can also use a tower or building near your city, such as the CN Tower or the Empire State Building.)

(continued)

Stair Step-Ups   *(continued)*

» To include more variation for this activity and to improve the effectiveness of the exercise, encourage the students to travel up the steps in various but safe ways. Here are some examples:
- Walk up stairs, single step.
- Walk up stairs, two steps.
- Hop up stairs, two feet, single step.
- Hop up stairs, right foot, single step.
- Hop up stairs, left foot, single step.
- Take side-to-side single steps.
- Take side-to-side double steps.
- Do single crossover steps to the left.
- Do single crossover steps to the right.

» The teacher stands at the top of the stairwell holding a sign indicating the next type of movement students should do when traveling up the stairs. Students will always walk down the stairs, hold on to the railing, and travel on the right-hand side.

TRIANGLE TAG

)) OBJECTIVE

For the person who is "it" to tag the target player

)) PLAYERS

Any number, although a larger group of players may work better

)) EQUIPMENT

One pinny per group

)) SETUP

1. The game should be played in a large, open area.
2. Organize the players into groups of four.
3. One player in each group is designated as the target and wears a pinny.

)) INSTRUCTIONS

1. Three of the group members hold hands, and one of these three is designated as the target (by a pinny).
2. The fourth group member is "it" and cannot enter the triangle.
3. "It" tries to tag the target, and the triangle moves around and shifts to keep away from the person who is "it."
4. "It" cannot reach across the triangle and must tag the target on the back.
5. When the target is tagged, a new triangle is formed with a new target, and a new player is "it."

)) VARIATIONS

» Players who are "it" can tag any target in any group.
» Instead of holding hands, players hold onto a pool noodle between them; the "it" holds a pool noodle with which she must hit the target (cannot hit across the triangle).

» OBJECTIVE

To score the required number of points

» PLAYERS

Groups of three or four

» EQUIPMENT

- » One hula hoop per group plus one more
- » 8 to 12 tennis balls

» SETUP

1. This activity is an excellent sprinting activity. Although only a few players are active at one time, this is a fast-moving game in which the players work very hard for a short period of time, have a short rest, and then are active again.

2. Take the players to the gymnasium or to an open area outside. Place a hula hoop (nest) in the center of the playing area with the other nests about 10 to 15 feet (3 to 5 m) from the center, although spacing the hoops farther apart is an option where space permits. Place 8 to 12 tennis balls (eggs) in the center nest for 6 or 7 teams (use fewer balls for fewer teams).

3. Divide the players into equal teams, and have each team stand in a line behind one of the nests around the circle.

» INSTRUCTIONS

1. On the signal to begin, the first runner runs to the center nest, picks up a tennis ball (egg), and brings it back to his nest. The egg must be placed (not thrown) into the nest. If it bounces out, the egg breaks and must be given to the leader. Once the egg is in the nest, that player goes to the back of the line, and the next person runs.

2. The players return to the center nest *or* to another team's nest to grab another egg. Teams cannot prevent other players from taking the eggs from their nests, but they can shout encouragement and advice (such as where to take an egg from) to their own team members.

3. When one team has three eggs in its nest, that round is over and the team gets a point. All eggs are quickly returned to the center, and the game begins again.

Safety Tip

Caution players about bumping heads when bending down to pick up objects.

» *VARIATIONS*

- » Numbering: Each player has a number, and the leader calls out the number of the player who must run. That runner continues to run until the leader calls out a new number.

- » Use stuffed animals (call it "Animal Rescue"), or clothespins or beanbags in place of tennis balls.

- » Soccer Dribble: Use soccer balls instead of small objects, and have the runners dribble the ball to their hoop and trap it inside their hoop before the next runner goes.

Adapted, by permission, from Ontario HPE Curriculum Support, Ophea.

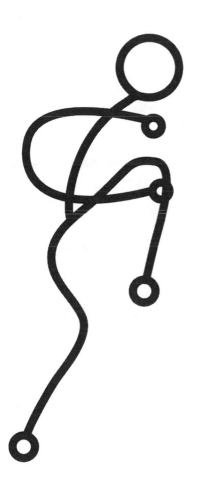

FITNESS CIRCUIT

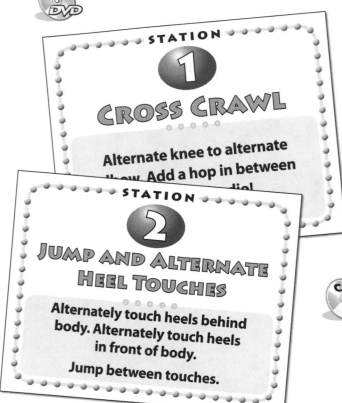

OBJECTIVE

For the players to do the activities on the instruction cards at each station

STATION 1
CROSS CRAWL
Alternate knee to alternate elbow. Add a hop in between for more cardio!

STATION 2
JUMP AND ALTERNATE HEEL TOUCHES
Alternately touch heels behind body. Alternately touch heels in front of body.

Jump between touches.

PLAYERS

Any number

EQUIPMENT

Station instruction cards printed from DVD-ROM

SETUP

Set up stations around the classroom, and distribute the players evenly at each station.

INSTRUCTIONS

Have players move from station to station to do each activity. Stations are listed in the following table.

SUGGESTED MUSIC

Use 30-second clips from the *Everybody Move!* CD.

Adapted, by permission, from Ontario HPE Curriculum Support, Ophea.

Station	Activity
Station 1: Cross Crawl	Alternate knee to alternate elbow. Add a hop in between for more cardio!
Station 2: Jump and Alternate Heel Touches	Alternately touch heels behind body. Alternately touch heels in front of body. Jump between touches.
Station 3: Jump and Twist Sideways	Jump and twist. Jump to the side and back.
Station 4: Jumping Jacks	Jump—arms out and feet out. Jump together. Keep knees flexed. How many can you do?
Station 5: Jogging on the Spot With Arm Punches	Punch in front, punch to the side, punch up. Raise your knees.
Station 6: Lunge	Lunge, then switch legs. Push off front leg back to standing. Add an arm action.
Station 7: Jogging on the Spot With Arm Crosses	Arms outstretched to sides at shoulder height. Cross your arms low and high. Raise your knees.

Ensure players have enough room to move and will not bump into furniture or each other. Outline the expected safety practices to players before beginning.

» VARIATIONS:

» Here is another set of stations:

Station	Activity
Station 1: Tuck Jumps	Do as many as you can. Jump as high as you can. Tuck as tight as you can. Beat your own record.
Station 2: Fireworks	Jump up and create a different pose each time.
Station 3: Hopping	Do 10 hops on one foot, 10 on the other, 10 on both, and repeat.
Station 4: Wake Up Sleeping Giant	Lie down and stand straight up. Repeat.
Station 5: Pushover	Stand facing the wall, pushing against it, trying to make the room bigger.
Station 6: Walk the Plank	Walk along a line on the floor, skip along it, and hop along it.
Station 7: Peek-a-Boo	Stand back to back with a partner, and take two giant steps forward. Bend at the waist, look between your legs, and wave at your partner. Then walk back to your partner on your hands and feet in straddle position.

(continued)

Fitness Circuit *(continued)*

» Here is one more set of stations:

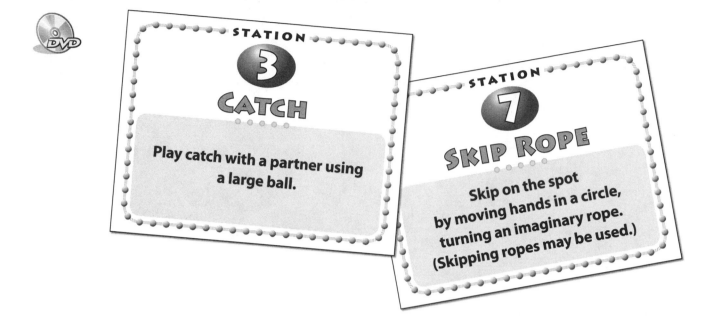

Station	Activity
Station 1: Hula Hoop	Place a hoop around your waist and move your hips in a circle to keep the hoop in the air.
Station 2: Beanbag Toss	Throw a beanbag into a hoop about 6 feet (2 m) away. Then run to retrieve the beanbag and repeat as many times as possible, as if doing a shuttle run. Count how many times the beanbag lands in the hoop.
Station 3: Catch	Play catch with a partner using a large ball.
Station 4: Popcorn	From a tuck position, with hands touching the floor, jump up and down as many times as possible.
Station 5: Skier Hops	Hop side to side while pushing fisted hands back (triceps curls) with each jump.
Station 6: Pull Up Your Shorts	Pretend to pull up shorts while alternately kicking each leg back (hamstring curls).
Station 7: Skip Rope	Skip on the spot by moving hands in a circle, turning an imaginary rope. (Skipping ropes may be used.)

CHUCK THE CHICKEN

» OBJECTIVE

To obtain as many points as possible by running laps around teammates

» PLAYERS

Any number, although a large group (e.g., a class) is best

» EQUIPMENT

A rubber chicken

» INSTRUCTIONS

1. Divide players into two teams. Both teams start at one end of the gym in their respective lines.
2. Team A throws the rubber chicken.
3. Team B runs after it, gets in a line, and the first person to grab it passes the rubber chicken over and under until it reaches the end of the line.
4. Meanwhile, the player from team A who threw the chicken has to run around her team. One lap equals one point.
5. When team B reaches the end of their line, it is their turn to throw the rubber chicken, and team A has to run after it.

» VARIATIONS

- » For older children, playing in a more open area makes the game more challenging.
- » To change the difficulty level of the game, the object being thrown can be substituted for another object more relevant to the age group.

HALLWAY SPEEDSKATING

» OBJECTIVE

To be the first to complete the hallway or gymnasium speedskating race

» PLAYERS

Any size group (activity can be performed individually or in teams, depending on the size of the group)

» EQUIPMENT

Each team or person needs at least two pieces of paper. Extra paper may be given in case the paper tears during the race.

» SETUP

1. Give each team two pieces of paper and get them to line up in the hallway.
2. Designate a finish line or turnaround point at some point in the hallway.

» INSTRUCTIONS

1. Team members place one piece of paper under each foot.
2. On the signal to begin, players must skate down the hallway to the designated point before turning around and skating back to their team.
3. The next player in line places his feet on the paper and repeats the relay.
4. A team wins when all players on that team have completed the relay.
5. Be sure to check that ink from the paper does not wear onto the floor if using recycled paper.

» VARIATION

After the speedskating, have a snowball fight with the crumpled-up paper to see who can get the most snowballs on the other side before the leader calls out, "Stop." Then have the players take shots at hitting the recycling box with the crumpled paper.

CHAPTER 5

Outdoor Activities

The great outdoors is a great place for children to play and to get some fresh air and vitamin D. Most tag games will work outdoors and many ball games as well. This chapter offers some creative activities that are also great fun. Follow the Fish is like follow the leader, and the leaders use different locomotion patterns as they move about the playing space. Disc Golf Race is a speed game that involves accuracy of throwing plastic discs. Doghouse is just plain madness as upset dogs go barking and jumping back to their doghouses. Vita Parcours is an outdoor fitness circuit. We have also included some fun outdoor tag games to play.

FOLLOW THE FISH

>> **OBJECTIVE**

For players to follow the movement pattern of the leader of their group

>> **PLAYERS**

Any number of groups of four to eight

>> **EQUIPMENT**

One rubber fish (or chicken or ball) per group

>> **SETUP**

1. Groups are scattered in the playing area, with each person in the group standing behind the next player in the group.
2. The first person in the line holds a bass.

>> **INSTRUCTIONS**

1. On the signal to begin, the first person in each line moves around the playing area in her chosen way (galloping, skipping, hopping, marching, or whatever safe way she wishes). The rest of the group follows their leader.
2. When the leader calls out, "Pass the fish!" the person with the fish gives it to the next person in line and then goes to the back of her line. The new fish holder leads the group around the space with a new movement pattern.

>> **VARIATION**

The leaders of each group only pass the fish when the instructor calls, "Pass the fish!"

DISC GOLF RACE

» OBJECTIVE

To see how quickly and with the fewest shots players can complete the golf course

» PLAYERS

Any number of pairs

» EQUIPMENT

- » One flying disc per pair of players
- » Recording sheet (photocopy one for each pair) (optional)

» SETUP

Divide the class into pairs, and give each pair a flying disc and a list of outdoor targets (e.g., the slide, the garbage can by the front doors, the fifth fencepost on the west fence, the drinking fountain, the four square game, the basketball hoop).

» INSTRUCTIONS

1. Players can hit the targets in any order they wish, but they may not carry the flying disc any distance. They must always throw it toward their destination.

2. Pairs take turns throwing the flying disc. One player throws, and the next picks it up from where it landed and throws it again.

3. Players play the game as a race against the others, with the number of throws not as important as how quickly they can hit every target. This can be recorded on a scorecard or mentally tracked (good practice for mental math!).

» VARIATIONS

- » Count the number of throws it takes to hit every target—the fewest throws wins.
- » Work on both speed and accuracy. Players can work on having both a low time and a low number of throws and then try to beat their own record.

Adapted, by permission, from Ontario HPE Curriculum Support, Ophea.

DOGHOUSE

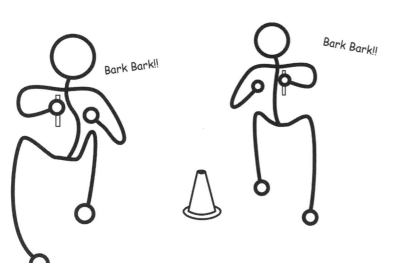

OBJECTIVE

To be the dog that never gets caught and sent back to the doghouse

PLAYERS

Any number

EQUIPMENT

» Popsicle sticks (equal numbers of four colors)
» Four pylons

SETUP

1. Play on a field, and have well-established boundaries. Give every player a Popsicle stick, and have sticks of four different colors. Each color represents a different color of dog. For example, players with red sticks are red dogs.
2. Each color is assigned a corner of the playing area, which is marked off by a pylon. This corner is that color's doghouse.

Bark Bark!!

Bark Bark!!

Bark Bark!!

INSTRUCTIONS

1. All the players run around the field, mingling with other dogs, holding their popsicle sticks in front so other players can see their colors. The leader yells out a color, and everyone with a stick that color is now "it."
2. When a player is tagged by someone who is "it," he must go back to his doghouse where he jumps up and down, barking.
3. When the leader calls out another color, the "its" change, and all the dogs are let out of their houses.
4. For increased activity and excitement, two colors can be called at once.

VARIATIONS

» Begin Doghouse as a walk, then skip, then gallop, then run. Gradually build up the players to running.
» Another variation is to time each group of dogs to see how quickly they can send everyone to their doghouses.

Adapted, by permission, from Ontario HPE Curriculum Support, Ophea.

CAPTURE THE FLAG

» OBJECTIVE

To capture all of the opposing team's flags

» PLAYERS

Works best with a large number of participants

» EQUIPMENT

- » Flags
- » Two sets of different-colored pinnies
- » Eight pylons

» SETUP

1. Divide a large field in two.
2. Divide the players into two equal teams. Each team goes to its side of the field.
3. Each team places its flags around its half of the playing area.
4. Teams use pylons to construct a 10-foot (3 meter) square "jail" somewhere on their half of the playing area.

» INSTRUCTIONS

1. Players must try to locate and obtain their opponents' flags.
2. If a player is touched on the other team's half, she must go to jail.
3. To be set free, a teammate must enter the jail and tag the teammate who is being held prisoner.
4. The game is over when one team captures all of the other team's flags.

» VARIATIONS

- » Participants could play the game tied together with a partner.
- » For cross-curricular links, write equations or trivia on the flags. Teams must take the flag to the instructor to test their knowledge. Teams must answer the questions on each flag they capture. All answers must be correct to win.
- » Sport Capture the Flag: Instead of flags, use balls. Players must return to their side by passing the ball back and forth in short passes with a partner.

VITA PARCOURS
(WAY OF LIFE; A JOURNEY)

» OBJECTIVE

To complete the Vita Parcours course

» PLAYERS

Any number

» EQUIPMENT

Laminated cards

» SETUP

Vita Parcours was invented in 1968 by architect Erwin Weckemann. It consists of an outdoor designated walking or jogging circuit with 10 to 20 designated stops. At each of the stopping places, spaced an equal distance apart (approximately 80 to 325 feet, or 25 to 100 meters), a laminated card or plaque instructs participants to perform a specific exercise that is repeated from 2 to 20 times—the hardest near the beginning of the course and the less difficult, relaxing ones scheduled toward the end. Stations may have several exercises to choose from, some of which are also different levels of difficulty. At some of the stops, appropriate playground equipment may be used. The participants' pulse rate should rise by the time they reach the finish.

» INSTRUCTIONS

Vita Parcours fitness circuits give participants the opportunity to exercise to improve their fitness at their own level and personal circumstances, at whatever time suits them. Jogging or brisk walking between stations improves cardiovascular endurance. Every circuit features different exercises aimed at improving participants' muscular strength, muscular endurance, and flexibility. Stimulating fitness challenges or wellness stations can be posted on cone boards, walls, windows, trees, fences, playground equipment, and so on. Participants can also wear pedometers to track their steps and help increase their activity level.

Regular physical activity in nature is good for participants' physical and psychological well-being and will encourage them to be physically active in their leisure time, in the fresh air. This exercise craze can also be referred to as the "green gym in the playground."

Suggested stations:

Shoulder rolls, forward 10 times and backward 10 times

Big arm circles, forward 10 times and backward 10 times

Jumping jacks or chicken jacks, 20 times

Wall squat for 20 seconds

Squats, 20 times

Cross crawl, 15 times each side

Pulling weeds, 20 times (hamstring curls)

Heel digs (push arms forward), 20 times

High knee lifts, 15 times each leg

Lunges, 15 times each leg

Calf lifts, 15 times

Mountain climbers, 20 times

Jump and twist, 20 times

Speed-boxer skips, 20 times

Leg abduction and adduction, 15 times each leg (bring leg out to side, then bring legs together)

Tae Bo kicks, 20 times each leg

Partial curl-ups, 15 times (on grass or mat)

Push-ups, 10 times (on grass or mat), or wall push-ups, 10 times

Step-ups, 15 times each leg (on stairs, bench, or playground beam)

Jumping rope, 20 times (real or pretend skipping rope)

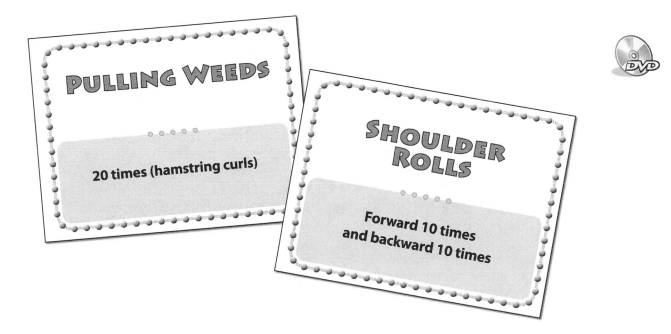

PULLING WEEDS

20 times (hamstring curls)

SHOULDER ROLLS

Forward 10 times and backward 10 times

BEANBAG TAG

OBJECTIVE

To avoid being tagged while keeping a beanbag on your head

PLAYERS

Any number

EQUIPMENT

- One beanbag per player
- A pool noodle for each "it"
- Four pylons to mark playing area

SETUP

1. Designate a playing area. If outside, mark the area with pylons.
2. Hand out one beanbag to each player.

INSTRUCTIONS

1. All players place a beanbag on top of their heads.
2. On the signal to begin, players walk briskly around the playing area, trying to avoid being tagged by the people who are "it."
3. If the beanbag falls off, the player must freeze. In order to be "unfrozen," another player must come and place the beanbag back on the player's head, without losing his own beanbag.

VARIATION

Play any tag game with a beanbag on top of players' heads to slow the pace down and increase the fun.

TRAIN TAG

» OBJECTIVE

For each team to try to attach to another team, while avoiding being caught by opposing teams (the persons on the back of the final train are the winners)

» PLAYERS

Any number of groups of three or four

» EQUIPMENT

Four pylons to mark playing area

» SETUP

1. Designate a playing area.
2. Members of each group form a train by placing their hands on the teammate in front of them.

» INSTRUCTIONS

1. On the signal to begin, the front of each train must try to attach to another train.
2. At the same time, the back of the train should try to avoid having another train attach to them.
3. Once two trains have joined, they work together to try to attach to other trains.

CHAPTER 6

Themed Activities

Certain times of the year and certain parts of the curriculum lend themselves to a series of games around a particular theme. This chapter provides a variety of games centered on themes.

Some of the games involve familiarizing the players with countries, as in Walk Across Your Country and Around the World Fitness Relay. Other games deal with the Olympic theme, such as Winner's Olympics and Summer Olympics. Some themes revolve around the seasons, such as Fall Frenzy, Celebrate Winter, Uncrate the Sun, and Spring Energy. Other themes include Valentine's Day, Survivor Fitness, and Heart Smart.

These themes are meant to whet your appetite. As you progress through different units while teaching throughout the year, challenge your students to create some fun and active theme games to add to your units of study.

WALK ACROSS YOUR COUNTRY

» *OBJECTIVE*

To add up distance walked or run in an attempt to "cross your country"

» *PLAYERS*

Any number

» *EQUIPMENT*

Map of country

» *SETUP*

1. Post a huge map of your country in a central location of the school.
2. Create a tally sheet with the following information for each class:

   Leader's name

   Number of players

   Total laps

   _____ laps = 1,000 feet (or 300 m)

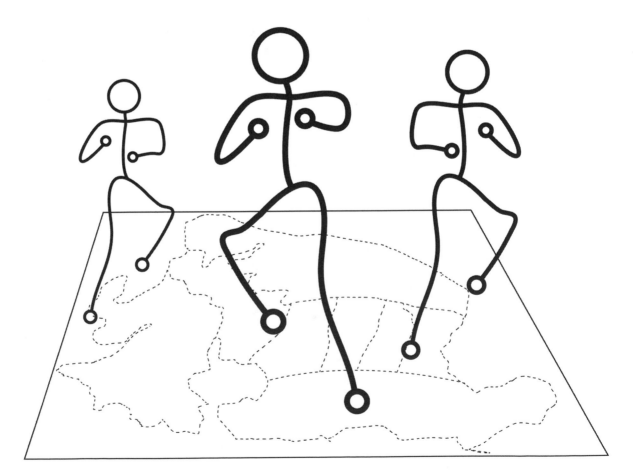

>> *INSTRUCTIONS*

1. Walk, jog, or speed-walk a designated measured route.
2. Players go as a group any time during the day.
3. Complete and hand in the tally sheet each day.
4. Tally total distances for the school.
5. Calculate and post results on the map to chart the progress.

>> *VARIATION*

You may need to supply rain routes such as in the gymnasium, around the halls, or in a covered area.

WINNER'S OLYMPICS

» OBJECTIVE

To participate in the 20 events of the Winner's Olympics

» PLAYERS

Any number

» EQUIPMENT

Station sheets printed from DVD-ROM

» SETUP

Place station sheets around the room, and divide the players around the stations.

» INSTRUCTIONS

1. On the signal to begin, players complete the assigned activity. "Hey gang! We're going to the Olympics! Prepare to win a medal! Start!"

2. On the signal to rotate, players move to the next station and complete that activity. Continue until all stations have been completed.

3. Some activities can be done sitting in chairs, and all can be done standing.

» SUGGESTED MUSIC

Use fast-paced music from the *Everybody Move!* CD. Song 21 ("Stadium Rock") works well for this activity.

⚬ Safety Tip

If this activity is done in the classroom, ensure that players stay in their own space.

Station	Activity
Station 1: Triathlon	Make swimming, bicycling, and running motions.
Station 2: Speedskating	Show arm and leg action of skating.
Station 3: Swimming	Show different strokes using arms and legs (front crawl, breaststroke, backstroke, sidestroke, butterfly).
Station 4: Slalom Skiing	Jump side to side, arms moving to opposite sides.
Station 5: High Jump	Jump as high as you can in the air.
Station 6: Archery	Pull one arm back while the other is straight; alternate.
Station 7: Diving	Pretend to dive off a diving board.
Station 8: Gymnastics	Hold a stork stand or other balance position.
Station 9: Baseball	Pretend to throw a ball. Use both arms.
Station 10: Canoeing	Alternate sides using paddling actions.
Station 11: Trampoline	Jump straight up and try making different shapes in the air (land with your feet together).
Station 12: Sprinting	Jog fast on the spot.
Station 13: Hockey	Pretend to take slap shots.
Station 14: Marathon	Do a slow, exaggerated running motion on the spot.
Station 15: Basketball	Pretend to dribble the ball with each hand.
Station 16: Sailing	Pretend to be the sail, blowing in the wind.
Station 17: Volleyball	Jump up and volley the ball over the imaginary net.
Station 18: Soccer	Dribble an imaginary ball with your feet.
Station 19: Equestrian	Gallop and complete a series of high jumps while remaining on one spot.
Station 20: Cycling	Sitting on a chair or the floor, use pedal power!

SUMMER OLYMPICS

» OBJECTIVE

To participate in the events of the Summer Olympics

» PLAYERS

Any number

» EQUIPMENT

- » Station sheets printed from DVD-ROM
- » Balls or beanbags
- » Baton
- » Beach ball
- » Scooter boards

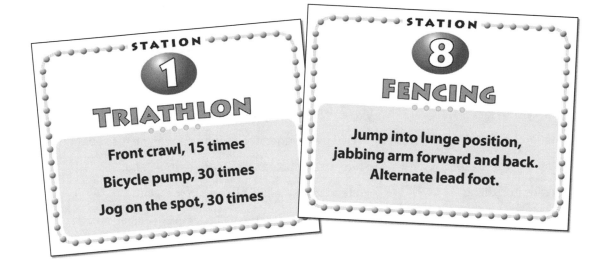

STATION 1

TRIATHLON

Front crawl, 15 times

Bicycle pump, 30 times

Jog on the spot, 30 times

STATION 8

FENCING

Jump into lunge position, jabbing arm forward and back. Alternate lead foot.

» SETUP

Place station sheets around the room, and divide the players around the stations.

» INSTRUCTIONS

The players circulate through stations in small groups and complete the following activities.

» SUGGESTED MUSIC

Play song 21 ("Stadium Rock") from the *Everybody Move!* CD.

Station	Activity
Station 1: Triathlon	Do 15 front crawls, do 30 bicycle pumps, and jog on the spot 30 times.
Station 2: Javelin Throw	Throw a pool noodle and fetch it.
Station 3: Relay	Holding an object in her hand (ruler, pool noodle), player 1 runs and skips around the room and then passes the baton to player 2, who does the same thing until everyone in the group has had a turn.
Station 4: Beach Volleyball	Volley or toss a ball five times in a row and then do eight push-ups (modified on knees or advanced full layout).
Station 5: Cycling	Lie on your back and do a bicycle pump—get hips off the floor.
Station 6: Rowing	Sit on the ground and simulate rowing as you make your way across the room (backward!) or to a designated area.
Station 7: Swimming	Move your arms in a front crawl motion as you move through the room.
Station 8: Fencing	Lunge forward while you jump on the spot.
Station 9: Surfing	Gallop and complete a series of high jumps while remaining on one spot.
Station 10: Boxing	Imagine an opponent in front of you. Hook, jab, punch—and keep those feet moving.
Station 11: Equestrian	Pretend to ride a horse and clear some jumps.
Station 12: Judges' Corner	Rest and score your peers in their events while you stretch.

FALL FRENZY

»» OBJECTIVE

To complete the various fall activities

»» PLAYERS

Any number

»» EQUIPMENT

- » Construction paper
- » A pair of gloves
- » Balloons

»» SETUP

The setup depends on the activity.

»» INSTRUCTIONS

Leaf Cutouts

1. Have every player make a leaf-shaped cutout with an activity written on it (e.g., jumping jacks, wall sit, toe touches).
2. Have everyone stand in a circle around the classroom. The students pass the leaves around until you say, "Stop." The players must then do the activity on the card they are holding until you say, "Pass." The students pass the leaves around the circle again.

Pumpkin Tag (played outside)

Play frozen tag. When a player is tagged, she must make the shape of a pumpkin. Give two or three players magic gloves that can touch pumpkins to activate them again.

Turkey Trot (played outside)

1. Divide the class into teams of five, and have every team line up.
2. The line begins to move about the playing area, walking in file formation. The last one in line runs to the front and becomes the leader as the line continues to move. When he gets to the front, he yells, "Go turkey!" or "Gobble gobble." The player at the back now runs to the front and becomes the new leader. The line continues to move, and the leader continues to change. Before long, the teams are constantly running.

Scarecrow

Yell out an activity for the class to do. When you yell, "Scarecrow," the players must stand like a scarecrow until you tell them what the next activity is.

Pumpkin Pass

Play the same game as Leaf Cutouts with pumpkin cutouts or orange balloons.

>> **OBJECTIVE**

To complete the various winter activities

>> **PLAYERS**

Any number

>> **EQUIPMENT**

Recycled paper

>> **SETUP**

The setup depends on the activity.

>> **INSTRUCTIONS**

Choose a different activity to do each day of the week to celebrate winter.

Snowball Storm

1. Divide the class and the classroom in half. Crumple recycled paper into balls.

2. On the signal to begin, each team throws "snowballs" onto the other team's half. Each team works to keep its own side clean. The team with fewer balls on its half of the room at the end of the game wins.

3. When finished playing, work together to clean up. Flatten the paper and return it to the recycling bin.

(continued)

Celebrate Winter   *(continued)*

Winter Circuit

Set up the classroom with a variety of stations, and have players spend a minute at every station.

Poinsettia Push-Ups

Jingle Bell Jog on the Spot

Snowflake Jump (jumping jacks)

Ski Jumps (side to side)

Candy Cane Kick (can-can)

Snowball Shuffle

1. Divide the class into two teams. Have each team form a conveyor belt by lying down so that one person's head and hands are by another person's feet.

2. Pile recycled paper "snowballs" at one end of each line.

3. Players move balls from one end of the line to the other by taking the ball in their hands, sitting up, putting it by their feet for the next person in line, and going back down for the next ball.

4. Teams work together to try to be the fastest to get all the balls to the other end.

5. Variation: Do it backward.

Winter Spelling

1. As you call out winter words (e.g., snow, snowflake, winter, cold, ski, skate), players try to form each letter with their bodies.

2. For consonants, players attempt to make their bodies into the shape of the letter.

3. For vowels, players do a specific action. For example (or use Fitness Spelling):

   A = reach up and then touch the ground

   E = twist jump

   I = jumping jack

   O = tuck jump

   U = arm punches

4. Variation: Have players make up their own vowel actions, or create a complete action alphabet.

Go Outside

1. Have a relay using a candy cane as a baton.

2. Make snowpeople.

3. Follow Frosty: Play follow the leader on the playground.

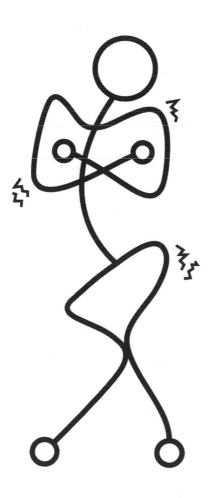

» ## OBJECTIVE

To complete various beach activities

» ## PLAYERS

Any number

» ## EQUIPMENT

- » Two hula hoops, one beach ball
- » Bucket of sand, one spoon, broom
- » Golf putter, golf ball, golf target
- » Three scooters
- » One Wiffle ball, some string
- » One hula hoop, dress-up clothes
- » Four flying discs

» ## SETUP

1. This is a game that the entire school can play, with each class going to the gymnasium at different times.

2. Set up stations in the gymnasium. Different grades come in at different times and compete within the grade. You can record scores to see who has the best score in the school. You can also measure how well you can do with an entire school or recreation group. Another option is to have no score but to have stations that are simply fun to do.

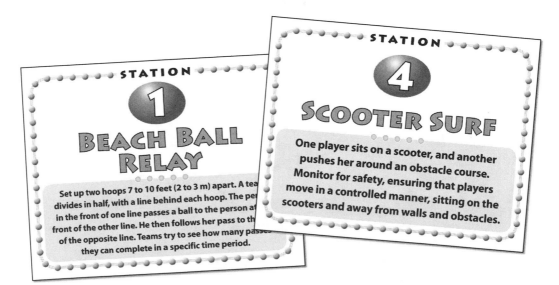

STATION 1 — BEACH BALL RELAY
Set up two hoops 7 to 10 feet (2 to 3 m) apart. A team divides in half, with a line behind each hoop. The person in the front of one line passes a ball to the person at front of the other line. He then follows her pass to the [back] of the opposite line. Teams try to see how many passes they can complete in a specific time period.

STATION 4 — SCOOTER SURF
One player sits on a scooter, and another pushes her around an obstacle course. Monitor for safety, ensuring that players move in a controlled manner, sitting on the scooters and away from walls and obstacles.

3. Divide each grade or group into teams, and have each team come up with a summer-themed name for themselves. For example, "Sandy Beach," "The Sweaty Armpits," or "SPF 15s."

4. Play music. Each team starts at one station and rotates through them all. Each station is 90 seconds.

Station	Activity
Station 1: Beach Ball Relay	Set up two hoops 7 to 10 feet (2 to 3 m) apart. A team divides in half, with a line behind each hoop. The person in the front of one line passes a ball to the person at the front of the other line. He then follows his pass to the end of the opposite line. Teams see how many passes they can complete in a specific time period.
Station 2: Sand Castle Relay	A team lines up behind a bucket with sand in it. One at a time, players take sand from that bucket and dump it into another bucket about 10 feet (3 m) away using only a spoon. Teams see how much sand they can move. This station requires a broom to periodically clean sand off the floor. As an alternative to sand, have players carry ping-pong balls, marbles, or other small items on a spoon.
Station 3: Mickey and Minnie Putting	Set up a small mini-golf putting green, using a plastic putter and practice balls and a box with a hole cut out. Teams see how many shots they can sink in the time period.
Station 4: Scooter Surf	One player sits on a scooter, and another pushes her around an obstacle course. Monitor for safety, ensuring that players move in a controlled manner, sitting on the scooters and away from walls and obstacles, keeping their hands off of the floor.
Station 5: Crab-Walk Kick	Suspend a Whiffle ball from a basketball hoop. Players line up behind a line and one by one walk to the ball in crab-walk position, kick it as hard as they can, and return to the back of the line.
Station 6: Scooter Swimming	Players lie on their bellies on a scooter and can use only their arms to move from one area to another. This can be done as a relay. Monitor safety, and remind players to tie hair back and to keep loose clothing and fingers away from scooter board and wheels.
Station 7: Dress-Up Relay (Sun Safety Relay)	Teams line up behind a start line; a pile of dress-up clothes lies in a hula hoop about 10 feet (3 m) away. The first player runs to the hoop, puts on an article of clothing, and runs back. He takes off that item for the next player in line to put on. The next player runs to the hoop and grabs another article of clothing, puts it on, and runs back. The third player in line puts on both the articles of clothing before going to get a new one. The game continues until all the clothes are gone or until everyone has had a turn. Teams see how quickly they can finish.
Station 8: Disc Fling	Players try to hit a target on the wall or a pylon on the ground. They must then retrieve their flying discs and throw them again from the starting point. Teams see how many times they can hit the target within the time period.

(continued)

Uncrate the Sun   *(continued)*

 » **SUGGESTED MUSIC**

» Try the Beach Boys, Jimmy Buffet, or any tropical or beach music.

» Use "sunny music" from the *Everybody Move!* CD, such as song 36 ("Jammin' Mon") or one of the Latin Mix songs 11-14.

Safety Tips

❋ *Ensure that areas involving sand are kept clean in order to avoid accidents as players move through.*

❋ *Ensure that players keep hair and clothing away from the floor when using scooters.*

CUPID'S ARROW

OBJECTIVE

To engage the whole school in a shared activity

PLAYERS

Any number

EQUIPMENT

Fitness card arrow

SETUP

Make an arrow or heart-shaped piece of paper, and attach a fitness card to it.

INSTRUCTIONS

1. Circulate the arrow around the school. The students in each class do the activity when the arrow comes to their class. When finished, they pass it on to the next class.

2. This game can be done for the whole Valentine's Day week; simply change the fitness activity daily.

Possible activities:

Two minutes of jumping jacks

Two minutes of sideways ski jumps

Forward and backward hops

Hula hoop twists

Stationary butterfly strokes

VARIATIONS

» Have more than one arrow. Classes can choose whether or not they want to do each activity when it comes to them. Track the activities, and post the number of activities done by each class.

» A good idea for Valentine's Day and the weeks around it is to post Jump Rope for Heart posters and posters for the Heart and Stroke Foundation.

STATION 2
FIRE-PIT PUSH-UPS

STATION 5
BEACH-BUM DIPS

Do three sets of 10 bench dips.

>> **OBJECTIVE**

To try to complete the Survivor stations

>> **PLAYERS**

Any number

>> **EQUIPMENT**

» Beanbags
» Pylons
» Skipping ropes

>> **SETUP**

1. Set up stations around the classroom or gymnasium, each named after an aspect of the television show *Survivor*.

2. Have players start at different stations and rotate.

Station	Activity
Station 1: Tribal Council	Do partial bent-knee curl-ups (crunches) as slowly as you can.
Station 2: Fire-Pit Push-Ups	Do as many push-ups as you can.
Station 3: Reward Running	Run on the spot.
Station 4: Tree Mail Tuck Jumps	Do tuck jumps.
Station 5: Beach-Bum Dips	Do three sets of 10 bench dips.
Station 6: Island Beanbag Race	Shuttle beanbags from one pile to another.
Station 7: Campground Crab Walk	Crab-walk around a series of pylons.
Station 8: Jeff's Jungle Jacks	How many jumping jacks can you do in a minute?
Station 9: Million-Dollar Marathon	Do this sequence as often as you can: 20 mountain climbers; lunge across room (back straight, knees over, not beyond, toes); jog back with high knees.
Station 10: Skip to Survive	Power skip.
Station 11: Rock Jump	Side-to-side jumps over lines, ropes, or beanbags.
Station 12: Survivor Stroll	Walk perimeter of the room for one minute to cool down. Note: This can be the last station for everyone. Another option is to set this station up a few times throughout the other stations, so that players have a few opportunities to rest.

»» *INSTRUCTIONS*

Players get one minute at every station, but give them about 20 seconds between stations to rotate and to figure out what to do. See Funky Moves starting on page 122 for descriptions of some of the activities.

»» *SUGGESTED MUSIC*

Use lively songs from the *Everybody Move!* CD, such as track 21 ("Stadium Rock").

HEART FITNESS CIRCUIT

DVD

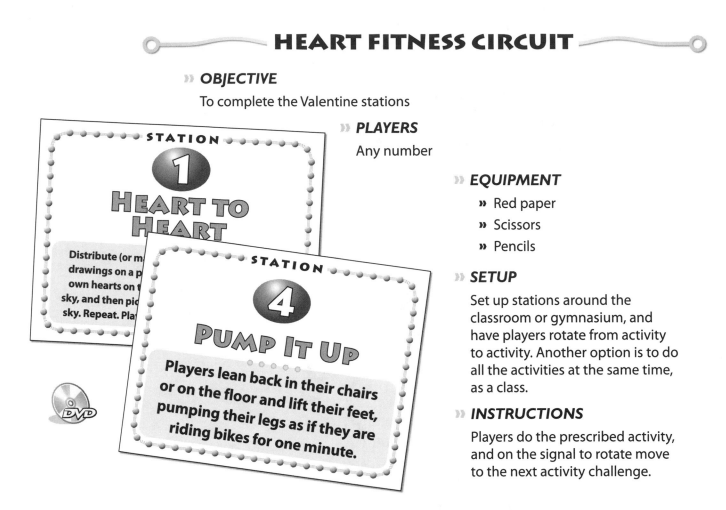

» OBJECTIVE

To complete the Valentine stations

» PLAYERS

Any number

» EQUIPMENT

- » Red paper
- » Scissors
- » Pencils

» SETUP

Set up stations around the classroom or gymnasium, and have players rotate from activity to activity. Another option is to do all the activities at the same time, as a class.

» INSTRUCTIONS

Players do the prescribed activity, and on the signal to rotate move to the next activity challenge.

Station	Activity
Station 1: Heart to Heart	Distribute (or make as a class) heart cutouts or drawings on a piece of paper. Players put their cutouts on the floor, stand up, point to the sky, and then pick up the heart and raise it to the sky. Repeat. Players do this as often as they can.
Station 2: Hopping Hearts	Players do two-foot jumps over a heart cutout on the floor as often as they can.
Station 3: Pass the Heart	The whole group jogs or moves on the spot. They pass a heart around the circle; as the heart comes to each student, she changes her type of movement.
Station 4: Pump It Up	Players lean back in their chairs and lift their feet, pumping their legs as if they are riding bikes for one minute
Station 5: Head Over Heels	Players work in partners about 10 feet (3 m) away from each other. One player stands with his legs apart. His partner runs toward him and crawls under his legs and then stands approximately 10 feet (3 m) away with legs apart. The players continue to switch roles and repeat as often as possible in two minutes.
Station 6: Cupid's Cardio	The whole group jogs or moves on the spot. When you call out, "Cupid's cardio," players call out, "Inside, outside, inside, outside," touching their ankles in front and behind their bodies.

SPRING ENERGY/ CHINESE NEW YEAR/EASTER EGG HUNT

» OBJECTIVE

For players to complete assigned activities

» PLAYERS

Any number

» EQUIPMENT

- » Plastic eggs or Chinese New Year envelopes
- » Small pieces of paper with activities written on them

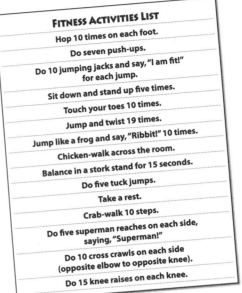

» SETUP

Use plastic eggs (available around Easter) or Chinese New Year money envelopes (available in January). Cut up a list of activities (see Fitness Activities List on the DVD-ROM), and place an activity in each egg or envelope. Scatter eggs or envelopes around the classroom or gymnasium (or in several egg baskets).

» INSTRUCTIONS

Players move around the room, opening eggs or envelopes and doing the activities. When they are finished with an activity, they put the paper back as they found it and move on to a different activity.

(continued)

Spring Energy/Chinese New Year/Easter Egg Hunt *(continued)*

»» *VARIATIONS*

» Players make their own list of activities. This way, there can be different activities for different skill levels and for specific units in physical education.

» Fortune Cookie Fitness: Play music and have the group follow the leader's instructions as they are announced. Inside the egg is a slip of paper, like a fortune, that describes the activity to be completed. Leaders take instructions from plastic eggs one at a time and read them aloud.

» Egg Toss: Partners face each other standing a few feet or meters apart. They throw the egg underhand to each other. Every time the egg is successfully caught, the thrower takes one step backward, thereby increasing the throwing distance. Players continue tossing the egg and stepping back until the egg is dropped. The partners then open the egg (if it hasn't cracked open already) and complete the activity together.

» Fit Flops: Purchase inexpensive flip-flops from a dollar store, and write different activities on the bottom of each flip-flop.

» Fit Mitts: Purchase inexpensive mittens from a dollar store, and place an activity that raises the heart rate inside each mitten (more ideas for activities can be found in Climbers and Sliders on page 59).

Ideas for exercise:

Hop 10 times on each foot.

Do seven push-ups.

Do 10 jumping jacks and say, "I am fit!" for each jump.

Sit down and stand up five times.

Touch your toes 10 times.

Jump and twist 19 times.

Jump like a frog and say, "Ribbit!" 10 times.

Chicken-walk across the room.

Balance in a stork stand 15 seconds.

Do five tuck jumps.

Take a rest.

Crab-walk 10 steps.

Do five superman reaches on each side, saying, "Superman!"

Do 10 cross crawls on each side (opposite hand, opposite knee).

Do 15 knee raises on each knee.

Do 15 gluteal kicks with each leg.

Do 10 shoulder rolls forward and 10 backward.

Balance on one foot for 15 seconds.

Do 10 stride jumps on each side and say, "Sunshine," each time.

Hop on both feet 10 times.

Do 10 touch earth, pat sky moves.

March for 20 seconds.

Do 15 raise the roof moves.

Do 10 crisscross jumps.

Do eight waves on each side.

Give yourself five hugs and say, "I am special," five times.

See Funky Moves starting on page 122 for descriptions of some of the activities.

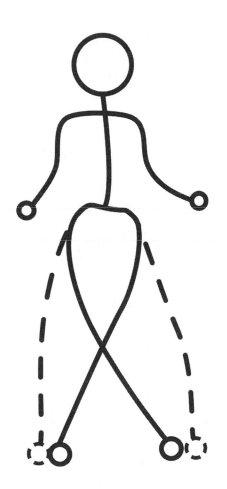

AROUND THE WORLD FITNESS RELAY

》 OBJECTIVE

To fly around the world closest to a preestablished time

》 PLAYERS

Any number

》 EQUIPMENT

- 》 Scorecards and pencils
- 》 Hoops or rope for airplanes

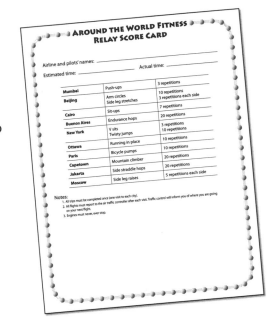

AROUND THE WORLD FITNESS RELAY SCORE CARD

Airline and pilots' names: _____

Estimated time: _____   Actual time: _____

Mumbai	Push-ups	3 repetitions
Beijing	Arm circles / Side leg stretches	10 repetitions / 3 repetitions each side
Cairo	Sit-ups	7 repetitions
Buenos Aires	Endurance hops	20 repetitions
New York	V sits / Twisty jumps	3 repetitions / 10 repetitions
Ottawa	Running in place	10 repetitions
Paris	Bicycle pumps	10 repetitions
Capetown	Mountain climber	20 repetitions
Jakarta	Side straddle hops	20 repetitions
Moscow	Side leg raises	5 repetitions each side

Notes:
1. All trips must be completed once (one visit to each city).
2. All flights must report to the air traffic controller after each visit. Traffic control will inform you of where you are going on your next flight.
3. Engines must never, ever stop.

》 SETUP

1. This activity is best if played on a playground or in a gymnasium.
2. Divide the class into teams of three or four, and give every team a scorecard (print these from the DVD-ROM). Every team chooses an airline name.
3. Each team is given a hoop or a rope, which is their airplane. When traveling, every member of the team must be touching the plane.
4. The leader is the air traffic controller (ATC), who stays in the middle of the playing area.

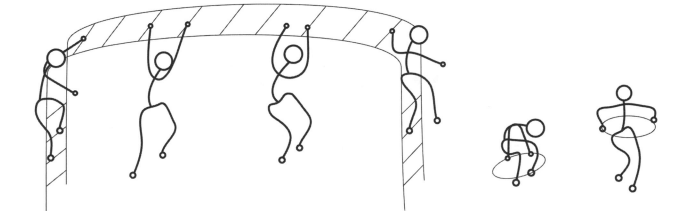

»» *INSTRUCTIONS*

1. Each team is to briefly visit each station once and predict the total time it will take them to complete each fitness activity.

2. Once all the teams have made their predictions, each airline is sent to its first city. At the whistle, each team will complete that fitness activity. When completed, the team will travel together, holding onto the plane, to the central airport where the ATC will tell the players what their next destination is to be according to the Air Traffic Controller Card.

3. Only one plane can land at the central airport at a time. If a team arrives when another airline has already landed, the players must circle the airport until it is their turn to land. All planes must remain in motion at all times. New teams arriving at the central airport line up behind the team before them, as the line circles around the ATC.

4. When at the central airport, the ATC will ask, "Where did you come from?" Depending on the group, instructions can be given by naming the city or by giving clues about the city's identification.

AIR TRAFFIC CONTROLLER CARD

Air Canada: Paris, Cairo, Beijing, Buenos Aires, New York, Ottawa, Capetown, Moscow, Mumbai, Jakarta

KLM: Cairo, Beijing, Buenos Aires, New York, Ottawa, Capetown, Moscow, Mumbai, Jakarta, Paris

Qantas: Beijing, Buenos Aires, New York, Ottawa, Capetown, Moscow, Mumbai, Jakarta, Paris, Cairo

Japan Airlines: Buenos Aires, New York, Ottawa, Capetown, Moscow, Mumbai, Jakarta, Paris, Cairo, Beijing

Air New Zealand: New York, Ottawa, Capetown, Moscow, Mumbai, Jakarta, Paris, Cairo, Beijing, Buenos Aires

Swiss Air: Ottawa, Capetown, Moscow, Mumbai, Jakarta, Paris, Cairo, Beijing, Buenos Aires, New York

Emirates: Capetown, Moscow, Mumbai, Jakarta, Paris, Cairo, Beijing, Buenos Aires, New York, Ottawa

Delta: Moscow, Mumbai, Jakarta, Paris, Cairo, Beijing, Buenos Aires, New York, Ottawa, Capetown

British Air: Mumbai, Jakarta, Paris, Cairo, Beijing, Buenos Aires, New York, Ottawa, Capetown, Moscow

Cathay Pacific: Jakarta, Paris, Cairo, Beijing, Buenos Aires, New York, Ottawa, Capetown, Moscow, Mumbai

5. The game continues until all teams have completed their flights around the world.

6. Congratulate the team whose time is closest to their estimated time. You can also recognize the team that finishes first.

OBJECTIVE

For players to complete the activities on the food group charts

PLAYERS

Any number

EQUIPMENT

Food group cards with suggested activities

LEAN MEATS AND ALTERNATIVES

Do 20 jumping jacks.

SETUP

Post food group activity cards around the room with activities to go with each food group (print cards from the DVD-ROM).

INSTRUCTIONS

1. Play a fast-paced song, and have players dance around the room while the music is playing.

2. When the music stops, players run to the food group closest to them and do the activity on that sheet until the music starts to play again. Players may not return to the same food group twice in a row.

Suggested food groups and activities:

Fruits and vegetables: modified push-ups

Low-fat dairy products: mountain climbers

Lean meats and alternatives: jumping jacks

Grain products: jogging on the spot

High-fat foods: pretending to sleep

Variety: combination of activities

This game works best when doing a unit on healthy eating.

SUGGESTED MUSIC

Use the get-moving songs from the *Everybody Move!* CD.

Safety Tip

Ensure players stay in their own space while moving around.

GET MOVING TO MUSIC!
Funky Moves and Group Routines

The three chapters in this section encourage us to help children move to music. Actually, moving to music often comes naturally, so these chapters are really about channeling those movements. Chapter 7 provides more than 100 dance moves that you can use to help understand routines we have choreographed or to have students create their own routines. You can print these moves on cards from the DVD-ROM. Chapter 8 provides detailed instructions for the routines on the *Everybody Move!* DVD-ROM. Chapter 9 provides similar instructions and cue sheets for music that children love listening to and dance steps that they love doing. These three chapters are about dancing, but for some who might find dance intimidating or for some reason not accepted by your students or community, think of this section as simply enjoying moving to music.

CHAPTER 7

Move It to the Beat— Actions for Music

There are an infinite number of dance moves in the world. In this chapter we note and describe more than 100 of them. The funky moves are arranged in such a way that they can easily be printed from the DVD-ROM, laminated, and then cut into individual cards and used by dancers to create their own routines. They are listed alphabetically so that you can refer to this chapter for a more complete description of the moves when you get to the routines in chapters 8 and 9.

Following are some activities you can do using the dance cards.

• **Dance Cards**—The objective is for students to create new and innovative dances using the funky moves on dance cards. Any number of students can do this activity at one time. All you need are the dance cards from the DVD-ROM and a CD player to play the *Everybody Move!* CD. Begin by giving each student a dance card. Play some music with a strong beat, such as "Marching Circus." Each dancer learns her dance to 8 beats and then repeats the activity. Dancers then find a partner and teach each other their move. Together they create 16 beats of dance that they repeat. Combine pairs into groups of four, and put actions together to create a series of eight-count moves for a total of 32 beats. Repeat the moves. Participants practice their long routines and teach them to the class.

Use songs from the *Everybody Move!* CD, such as "Marching Circus." As a variation, once groups have learned their music, put on different music and see if they can dance their routines to the new music.

• **The Same but Different**—Select 6 to 10 funky moves, and give each group the same dance cards. Have them work together to combine them into a routine. After giving participants time to practice, have the groups show their routines. Each group will demonstrate their own style.

• **Cross-Pollination**—Have participants work together in groups to create routines using moves from the Funky Moves list. After working together for a while, select one student from each group to move to the next group. She becomes their coach, watching what has been created so far and providing feedback based on her original experience in her original group. The coach then joins a new group and works with them to further develop their routine. Cross-pollination can take place a number of times, thus providing input and suggestions for routine development.

• **Half and Half Show**—After participants have developed their routines in small groups, have several groups show their work to the rest of the class. Having several groups perform at the same time diminishes the spotlight on groups who may be less comfortable performing in front of other students. You can encourage participants who are observing to make comments about the positive things they see.

• **Mix It Up**—Participants learn a routine together using the funky moves on the dance cards. In a small group, they practice the routine and then change it to make it their own by using different elements of dance. For example, they may change the formation, timing, or levels. They may echo moves, repeat them, or adjust the sequence. Post suggestions on the wall to give participants ideas of what they may consider varying.

FUNKY MOVES

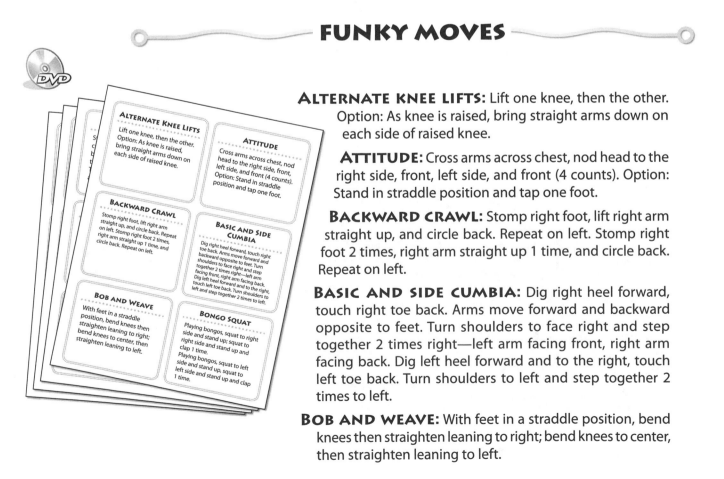

ALTERNATE KNEE LIFTS: Lift one knee, then the other. Option: As knee is raised, bring straight arms down on each side of raised knee.

ATTITUDE: Cross arms across chest, nod head to the right side, front, left side, and front (4 counts). Option: Stand in straddle position and tap one foot.

BACKWARD CRAWL: Stomp right foot, lift right arm straight up, and circle back. Repeat on left. Stomp right foot 2 times, right arm straight up 1 time, and circle back. Repeat on left.

BASIC AND SIDE CUMBIA: Dig right heel forward, touch right toe back. Arms move forward and backward opposite to feet. Turn shoulders to face right and step together 2 times right—left arm facing front, right arm facing back. Dig left heel forward and to the right, touch left toe back. Turn shoulders to left and step together 2 times to left.

BOB AND WEAVE: With feet in a straddle position, bend knees then straighten leaning to right; bend knees to center, then straighten leaning to left.

BONGO SQUAT: Playing bongos, squat to right side and stand up; squat to right side and stand up and clap 1 time. Playing bongos, squat to left side and stand up, squat to left side and stand up and clap 1 time.

BOX STEP: Step forward on right foot, cross left foot over right, step back with right, open out to the side again with the left. The opposite is acceptable as well.

BOXER SHUFFLE: With feet shoulder width apart, bounce lightly back and forth from right foot to left foot.

BROADWAY CHA-CHA: Dig right heel diagonally across left foot, tap right toe diagonally behind left foot to right side, and cha-cha 3 times on the spot. Dig left heel diagonally across right foot, tap left toe diagonally behind right foot to left side, and cha-cha 3 times on the spot. Arms move opposite to legs.

BUTTERFLY ARMS: Circle arms out and above head, hands crossed above head. Lower arms to front, crossing slightly at bottom.

CALYPSO CROSSOVER: Step left foot forward over right with a hop while curling right foot toward seat, with **pulling weeds** arms. Step back on right, then left. Step right foot forward over left with a hop while curling left foot toward seat, with **pulling weeds** arms. Step back on left, then right.

CALYPSO STOMP: Stomp left foot forward over right with a hop while curling right foot toward seat. Pull horizontal arms toward chest on 1, 2 and face front and slap sides on 3, 4. Stomp right foot forward over left with a hop while curling left foot toward seat. Pull horizontal arms toward chest on 5, 6 and face front and slap sides on 7, 8.

CAN-CAN: With your inside arms over each other's shoulders (or hands on waist), jump on both feet, lift right knee up while hopping on left; jump on both; kick right leg to left side while hopping on left; jump on both. Repeat with left leg.

CHA-CHA: Start with feet together. Step diagonally forward to left onto right foot; transfer weight to that foot; rock back onto left foot; step right foot back beside left; lift left, right, left (say, "Forward, back, cha cha cha"). Repeat with left foot.

CHARLESTON: Step on right foot, bring left foot forward and point toes in front. Step back on left foot, and point right toes behind. Repeat.

CHICKEN JACKS: Do jumping jacks, but tuck your hands under your armpits as if you are a chicken.

CHICKEN WALK: Walk in a circle on the spot with your hands in your armpits, flapping arms like a chicken (clucking or squawking is optional!).

CHUG STEP: With feet together, take bunny hops forward or backward.

CIRCLE STOMP: Pivot 1/4 turn right, stomp left foot forward 2 times, pivot right. Repeat three more 1/4 turns. Arm action: playing bongos. Repeat circle stomp to left.

CLAPPING SQUARE: With feet in a straddle position, clap hands high on the right (once), then high on the left, low on the right and low on the left (four beats in total).

CRISSCROSS JUMPS: With legs in a straddle position, jump up and before landing cross feet (e.g., right over left). Jump up again and uncross feet. Alternate feet.

CROSS CRAWL: Bring your right elbow and left knee together. Then bring your left elbow and right knee together. Variation: Funky Cross Crawl—the same as cross crawl but touch right, left, right, right then left, right, left, left.

CROSS JAB LEFT: Left arm crosses in front of your body and jabs to the right. **Cross jab right:** Right arm crosses in front of your body and jabs to the left.

CROSS KICK: Step on right foot; kick left foot across in front of your body over to the right. Repeat with the other side.

DIGS: Pretend to dig with a shovel left to right while stepping onto right foot. Pivot on right foot then repeat to left. Optional: Add a clap as direction is changing.

DISCO: Point right arm down across left hip, then stretch arm (finger pointed) diagonally up to right (repeat four or eight times). Repeat with left arm.

DOUBLE DOG LIFTS: Lift right leg, bent at a 90-degree angle, to right side 2 times. As leg rises, raise bent arms, fingers pointing to the ground as if attached to a string. Repeat on left side.

EGYPTIAN: Swivel to the right. Position right arm at a 90-degree angle palm up to the right, left arm at a 90-degree angle palm up to the left (two counts). Swivel to the left and repeat with opposite arms. Variation: Funky Egyptian—The same as Egyptian but move right, left, right, right then left, right, left, left.

EGYPTIAN DRAG: Step to right 4 times, dragging left foot with Egyptian arms. Step to left 4 times, dragging right foot with Egyptian arms.

EGYPTIAN SHUFFLE: Legs apart. Arm position: Start with right arm at 90-degree angle to right side, palm facing up; left arm is bent in front of body, parallel to floor, palm facing down. Pump to right. Left arm goes to 90-degree angle to left, palm facing up, and right arm parallel to floor, palm facing down. Pump to left. 4 times moving down, 4 times moving up

ELBOW POPS: With arms bent at 90 degrees, hands clenched close to body, lift elbows and shoulders up to right 1 time, to left 1 time, to right 2 times, and clap 2 times. Lift elbows and shoulders up to left 1 time, to right 1 time, to left 2 times, and clap 2 times.

ELEPHANT: Starting with feet together, step out to the side with right then left foot, and step them in right and left (out, out, in, in). Place hands at ears and as feet step out, elbows move out to the sides. As feet step in, bring elbows to center (representing large elephant ears).

FOOT FIRES: Run on the spot with your legs in a straddle position.

FUNKY CHICKEN: Put your hands on your waist and bring your elbows back (as if trying to touch elbows behind back). For added effect, bring knees together and apart at the same time.

FUNKY CROSS CRAWL: Same as **cross crawl**, but touch opposite elbow right, left, right, right, then left, right, left, left.

FUNKY EGYPTIAN: Same as **Egyptian**, but shuffle and go right, left, right, right and left, right, left, left (single, single, double).

FUNKY FISH: Put palms together with fingertips pointed at feet, and flick your fingers away from your body while moving them to the right three times; clap on fourth count. Repeat to the left.

FUNKY HIP-HOP: Step right foot to right, touch left foot beside right. Step left foot to left, touch right foot to left. Step together to right 2 times. Arm action: Push arms to side in opposite direction of legs. Step left foot to left, touch right foot beside left. Step right foot to right, touch left foot beside right. Step together to left 2 times. Push arms to side in opposite direction of legs.

FUNKY JACK: Jump to a straddle, jump feet together, jump to a straddle, and pause for a count (count one, two, three, pause), then jump feet together, jump to a straddle, jump feet together, and pause.

FUNKY KNEE LIFTS: Same as **knee lifts**, but lift right, left, right, right, then left, right, left, left (single, single, double).

FUNKY LEG CURLS: Standing on left foot, bend right knee and kick seat with heel 4 times while brushing right shoulder with left hand 4 times. Standing on right foot, bend left knee and kick seat with heel 4 times while brushing left shoulder with right hand 4 times.

FUNKY PULLING WEEDS: Same as **pulling weeds**, but kick buttocks right, left, right, right, then left, right, left, left.

FUNKY V-STOMP: Stomp right foot diagonally right, raising right arm straight up in direction of right leg; stomp left foot diagonally left, raising left arm straight up in direction of left leg; jog back 3 times.

THE GIVING: Stand with elbows bent (pointing down), palms facing shoulders. Chug right heel forward while straightening arms to right. Return foot to center and bend elbows back up. Repeat on left side.

GIVE MORE: The same as **the giving** but make it more pronounced by jumping into the chug, and bending at waist as arms straighten. Jump feet together as elbows bend back up.

GOING PLACES: Jog in place with knees high.

GRAPEVINE: Step out to right, cross left foot behind right, step out to right, then tap left foot beside right foot (or jump feet together). Repeat to left.

GRAPEVINE POINT: Grapevine with finger pointing while moving across front of body, arm extended.

GRAPEVINE WITH TURN: Step to right with right foot, and pivot on right foot 180 degrees clockwise (until facing backward); pivot on left foot 180 degrees clockwise (until facing forward), step left foot to right.

HAMSTRING CURLS: Stand in a straddle position and alternately bring heels up to buttocks.

HEEL CHUGS: Standing on left foot, dig right heel into the floor while arms push away (chest press). Standing on right foot, dig left heel into the floor, leaning back and pushing arms away ("Heel left chugs, say no to drugs"). Option: Push arms up (shoulder press).

HEEL CLICKS: Stand on toes with feet slightly apart, and click heels together and apart.

HEY YOU: Tap toe, point finger, and move arm up and down across your body, first with one arm, then with the other; put other hand on hip while not pointing.

HIT THE TABLE: Push palms down as if putting hands onto a table: right hand down in front of body, then left, then right hand behind body, then left.

HITCHHIKE: Holding your arm in front with thumb up, flick your thumb backward as your arm moves back four times (repeat on other side); alternatively, point your right thumb over your right shoulder, flicking it back two times. Repeat with left.

HOLE IN THE FENCE: Step side to side. While stepping sideways, duck your head as if moving through a hole in a fence. Your shoulders, arms, then rest of body follow your head as if moving through the hole. Repeat on the other side.

HOOK: Take a short power punch from the side of the body to the center, keeping the arm at or near 90 degrees. Switch sides.

JAB: Hands begin in a fist position, in front of the face or jaw. Punch right hand forward with flat part of knuckles while maintaining a straight-line alignment from hand to shoulder. Should be delivered in a "snapping" way without locking elbow. Switch sides.

JUMP AND SQUAT: Jump to a squat facing right side, hands on thighs; jump back to face front. Clap hands 2 times. Repeat to left.

JUMPING JACKS: Jump legs to a straddle position while raising arms to a V shape above your head. Jump legs together, bringing arms to side. Repeat.

KICK BUTT/GLUTEAL KICKS: Jog on the spot, with heels kicking your buttock.

KICK SQUATS: Kick right foot forward, kick left foot forward (opposite arms reach forward and backward). Squat right with **butterfly** arms (hands come together in front of chest, lift straight up when stepping out to side) and pull elbows down at 90-degree angle to side while squatting (biceps curl). Hands come back up together and pull down in front when feet come back together. Kick left foot forward, kick right foot forward, squat left with **butterfly** arms.

KICKS: Keeping legs straight, alternately kick legs to front (four or more beats), side, and back.

KNEE DRIBBLE: Step right foot forward over left and dribble 1 time with right hand; step back on right foot and dribble 1 time with right hand. Step together 2 times to right and dribble 2 times with right hand. Step left foot forward over right and dribble 1 time with left hand; step back on left foot and dribble 1 time with left hand. Step together 2 times to left and dribble 2 times with left hand.

KNEE LIFTS: Bend right knee up, reach hands under right leg, then lower leg and bring arms out to shoulder level. Lift left knee up, reaching hands under left leg, then lower leg and bring hands out again. Variation: Funky Knee Lifts—same as knee lifts except lift right, left, right, right then left, right, left, left.

KNEE PUMP: Step diagonally on right foot while pulling your left knee up in front of your body, then return to starting position.

KNEE SWING: Raise right knee while hopping on the left foot; jump, then raise left knee while hopping on the right foot.

KNEES UP: March, raising knees to waist height.

LASSO: With arm out to side, bent at elbow with fist facing up, rotate your forearm and wrist as if swinging a lasso (2 or 4 counts). Repeat on other side.

LAWN MOWER: Walk forward with both hands on an imaginary lawn mower, and then turn on the beat and go backward with only one hand on the mower. Your head can keep the beat with bobs or something else.

LION: Lift right foot and stomp it on the ground. At the same time, bend at the waist to the right, keeping your head down. Arms are out beside head, elbows bent, and palms down (2 counts). Snap up to standing with arms still beside head; draw shoulders and head back (2 counts). Repeat on left.

LOOK OUT: Lunge slowly to the right with your right hand in a horizontal peace sign moving across the front of the face (4 counts). Repeat to the left.

LUNGES: These can be done to the side or front. Start standing with feet together. To lunge forward, step forward on right leg, making sure your knee flexes over top of foot (not beyond). Keep back straight. Push off of right foot to return to standing position. Repeat on left leg. Side lunge is a step to the right, flexing right knee while keeping left leg straight. Push off of right leg to return to standing position. Repeat on left side.

MACHO MAN: Turn to the right and make a muscle with your right arm bent at elbow, fist up and turned toward face. Repeat to the left.

MAMBO: Step forward diagonally on right foot (in front of left foot), and transfer weight to that foot. Step back onto left foot, step on right foot beside left, then step on left to a steady 4-count.

MARCH: March on the spot, single or double time; widen legs apart to show attitude.

MARCH AND BREATHE: March feet while bringing arms up and out from waist overhead, 4 counts, then shake hands down in front, 4 counts. Breathe in as arms circle up, exhale as hands shake down.

MIRROR WIPE: With right palm out, wipe palm in one semicircular motion from center of body up and to the right. Repeat on left.

MONKEYS: Standing in a straddle position with knees slightly bent, make fists with your hands and hold arms straight out in front of your body. Alternately move arms up and down (one up, one down), keeping arms straight.

MOUNTAIN CLIMBERS: Starting in a push-up position on the floor, alternately bring knees up to the chest.

OPHEA HAND JIVE: Pull right elbow down with fists up two times; push right elbow out to the side two times; rotate right forearm in circular motion two times; make a wave action with right arm across body (2 counts) (cueing: down, down, out, out, circle, circle, wave, wave). Repeat with left arm. Continue with **Egyptian**: Swivel to the right. Position right arm at a 90-degree angle palm up to the right, left arm at a 90-degree angle palm up to the left (2 counts). Swivel to the left and repeat with opposite arms. Repeat on both sides. (Total: 32 counts)

PIVOT TURN: Step forward on right foot. Pivot to face back. Step forward again on right foot, and complete the pivot around to face front again.

PLYOMETRIC POWER LUNGE: Lunge with right leg in front. Jump up in the air and switch legs to land in lunge position, with the left leg in front.

POGO JUMP: With arms tight to your sides, jump up and down, keeping body as straight and aligned as possible.

POINT TO THE FOOT: Dig your right heel diagonally out to the right while pointing your finger at the foot. Bring your foot back, and repeat on the left. Look at your foot while pointing at it.

POLKA STEP: Hop with quick steps right, left, right, then left, right, left. Continue.

POWER LUNGE: Lunge forward on right leg, punching forward with left arm; bounce on second count. Repeat with left leg and right arm.

PULLING WEEDS: Standing in a straddle position, with arms extended down in front, bend elbows and pull fists up to chest, like an upward row. At the same time, bend right knee and kick seat with heel, straighten arms and legs then repeat on left side. (This move creates a rocking motion from left to right.) Variation: Funky Pulling Weeds—same as **Pulling Weeds**, but kick right, left, right, right, then left, right, left, left.

PULSING ARMS: Strong arms bent, hands clenched toward chest, pulsing action with forearms, alternating sides, moving forward 4 times and backward 4 times.

PUNCH IT OUT: Punch your arms forward—right, right, left, left, right, left, right, left (and other combinations).

PUNCHING SQUARE: With feet together, jump side to side. In time to the jumps, punch both arms up to right side, then punch to left side, then punch both arms down to right, then down to left (up right, up left, down right, down left).

RAINBOW ARMS: Lunge to the right side. Move right arm in a circle pattern overhead to rest on right knee. Option: Follow closely with the left hand. Repeat to left side.

RAISE THE ROOF: With palms facing toward the roof, push arms up 2 times to the left, two times to the right.

ROBOT: Step right foot diagonally to right with right foot leading 2 times with robot arms: straight arms extended in front of body, palms facing each other, alternately moving arms up and down. Step left foot diagonally to left with left foot leading 2 times with robot arms. March backward, stepping right, left, right, left, reaching under legs each time on counts 5, 6, 7, 8. Step left foot diagonally to left 2 times, step right foot diagonally to right 2 times, with robot arms. March backward left, right, left, right, reaching under legs each time.

ROCK SIDE TO SIDE: With legs in a straddle position, bounce the upper body over to the right side 2 times and then over to the left side 2 times.

ROCK STEP: Step diagonally forward on the right foot to the right side. Touch left toes down on the spot. Step back onto the left foot. Touch right toes on the spot. Your upper body moves down and back with the leg actions.

ROCKING HORSE: Step forward on the right foot; flex left leg (leg-curl action). Step back on the left foot; lift right knee up in front.

ROLL IT: Bend your arms at the elbows, and roll one forearm around the other. Roll in a circle (i.e., start at right hip, up to right shoulder, overhead to left shoulder, left hip, waist, and repeat), or roll in front of the chest.

ROLL UP AND DOWN: With legs together, roll your arms in front of your body all the way up high above your head and then back down low again.

SHAKER FISTS: Make a fist with each hand, and shake your fists and forearms 2 times forward and up to the right, then up to the left.

SHIMMY SHAKE: Walk forward four steps while leaning forward slightly, and quickly shake shoulders forward. Arms are straight and slightly behind. Alternatively, shake arms—like drying your lower back with a towel. Walk back four steps with palms out, facing down, shuffling hands back and forth. Option: Chug it back (jump backward) 4 times.

SHOULDER DIG: Step forward on right foot and dig right shoulder forward 2 times; jump up and **raise the roof** 2 times. Step forward on left foot and dig left shoulder forward 2 times; jump up and **raise the roof** 2 times.

SHOULDER SHRUG: Bring both shoulders up toward your ears, relax, and let shoulders drop down (or alternate one shoulder at a time).

SHUFFLE: Gallop sideways to the right for 4 counts. Repeat to the left.

SIDE JUMP: Jump to the right, landing on right foot. Tap left foot beside right foot. Repeat to left.

SIDE STRADDLE HOPS: Standing with legs shoulder-width apart, knees slightly bent and hands on thighs, hop to the right and then to the left.

SIDE TOUCH: Step side to side, touching the toe of one foot beside the opposite foot in a repeated sequence.

SIDE TOUCH AND SWING: Step side to side while swinging your arms.

SINGLE DOG LIFTS: Lift right leg to right side to 90-degree angle. Raise extended bent arms, fingers pointing to the ground, as leg rises (as if attached to a string). Lift left leg to left side to 90-degree angle, raising hands as leg rises.

SINK: Hold your nose with one hand; opposite hand is straight up with palm facing out. Bend your knees as you sink to the floor, with hand waving gently back and forth (4 counts).

SKIP IN PLACE: Step on your right foot and hop up on it. Repeat with left foot. Option: Swing arms as if turning a rope.

SLIDE: Step to the right and drag left foot to right. Move side to side or diagonally.

SPEED BAG: Roll the fists over one another as quickly as you can.

SPORTS MOVES: Move as if playing basketball, hockey, soccer, tennis, etc.

SPRINKLER: Put one arm out front and bend other arm at the elbow, placing your hand behind your neck, elbow pointing to the side. Jerk the bent arm toward the straight arm as if you are a watering the lawn with a sprinkler for 4 counts. Return elbow to start for 4 counts.

SQUISH THE BUG: Bend right knee up, step out to right on ball of foot. Exaggerate push and twist into the ground 3 times. Repeat on left.

STAR POINT: Point your right toe to the front, side, and back, then step beside your left foot. Repeat with left foot.

STEP HOP: Step to the right on your right foot and hop up on it. Repeat to the left.

STEP TOUCH: Step to the right on your right foot, then touch left foot beside right (2 counts) then step to the left on your left foot and touch the right foot beside left (2 counts).

STEP TOUCH BEHIND: Step to the right. Touch left foot behind right. Repeat to the left side.

STOMP: Stomp down with right foot, then repeat with left.

STRUT STEP: Walk four steps forward, rolling from heel to toe right, left, right, left (can also be done backward).

SUNRISE ARMS: Jog in place with straight arms moving up overhead (like jumping jack arms), with hands and fingers shaking. Move arms back down to sides and repeat (4 counts up, 4 counts down).

SWIVEL: With feet together, twist to the right, left, right, left.

TAE BO KICK (FRONT): Standing on left leg, bring your right knee up in front of your body. Extend your right foot straight out in front in a quick snapping motion (leading with the toe). Switch sides.

TAE BO KICK (SIDE): Standing on left leg, lift your right knee up to the side (parallel to the floor), extending the foot straight out to the side in a quick snapping motion (leading with the heel). Switch sides.

TAP IN: Standing in a straddle position, bring your right foot in and tap beside the left and back out to the side. Repeat with left.

TAP OUT: With feet together, tap right foot to right side and bring it back in. Repeat with left foot.

TO THE SKY: Stand with the feet in a straddle position. Reach up with both arms extended to the right, then bring them back to the front and clap; reach to the left, bring arms back to the front, and clap (4 counts).

TORSO TWIST: Standing with feet shoulder-width apart and knees slightly bent, turn your upper body side to side (waist-up movement only).

TRUNK: Place one hand over the other in front of your body. Slowly lift arms up above head and bend elbows as you bring them down.

TUCK JUMPS: Jump as high as possible and tuck your knees up to your chest.

TWISTY JUMPS: Jump and twist to alternate sides.

UP AND DOWN: Reach your arms up to the sky, then tuck down to touch the ground.

UPPERCUT: As your fist comes up from the center of your body, rotate your torso into a punch. As your arm comes up, the hip will pivot forward slightly for added power. Keep the punch close in front of your body. Switch sides.

V STEP: Begin with feet together. Step forward to the right with right foot, step sideways to the left with left foot, then step the right foot back to center followed by the left.

V JUMP: Begin with feet together. Jump forward to a wide squat, bringing hands up to a "stop" action. Jump back, feet together, clapping 2 times.

WALK AND CLAP: Walk forward three steps; jump and clap hands high on fourth count. Walk backward three steps; jump and clap low on fourth count.

WASHING WINDOWS: With palms facing out, move hands in small circles (together or alternating).

WAVE: With palm facing down and forearm parallel to the floor, move your arm in a wave motion across the body. Repeat with other arm. Option: Make up combinations such as one arm, the other arm, and then both arms at the same time in a 2 or 4 count.

THE WHY: Lift right knee up and open to the right while arms open up with palms up at shoulders (as if to say, "I don't know!" or "Why?"). Lower leg and bring arms to center and repeat to left.

WILDEBEEST STAMPEDE: With feet slightly apart, bend at waist and run rapidly on the spot with palms facing down in front.

WOUNDED DUCK: Jump with knees, fists, and toes facing in. Then jump with feet shoulder-width apart, knees, fists, and toes facing out. Repeat in and out jumping sequence.

CHAPTER 8

Ready-to-Use Routines— Dances and Routines on the DVD-ROM

The following routines use songs from the *Everybody Move!* CD. To further assist you, the routines are demonstrated on the DVD-ROM. Enjoy them, vary them, and keep everybody moving. The DVD-ROM can be shown while a leader is instructing the dance so that the dancers can follow either the leader or the DVD-ROM. Cue sheets are also provided for each dance on the DVD-ROM, and they can be transposed onto poster boards so the dancers know which dance move is coming up next. It is helpful for the leader to also cue the dancers before the next move is going to happen. Often leaders will give the DVD-ROM to some of the dancers to learn and then have them teach the dance to the other dancers. This is a great leadership opportunity.

Note that all directions are listed as L for left and R for right throughout the dances. All Funky Moves are in bold in the directions.

Routine Finder

Routine	Page number
Eddie the Razor	135
Motion Motion (Alley Cat)	136
Marching Circus	138
Gringo (Latin American)	140
Latinique	142
Dream Machine	144
Aerobics	146
Boxercise	149
Latin Mix: Mambo Jumbo	152
Latin Mix: Cumbia Urbana	154
Latin Mix: Reggaeton	157
Latin Mix: Lucky 6	159
Ethno Tension (African Routine)	161
Smile	162
Smile Yoga	163

Count	Instruction or pattern
16	**Shoulder shrugs** 8 times
16	**Attitude** 2 times
32	**Point to the foot** 16 times
32	**Funky fish** 8 times
32	**Ophea hand jive**
32	**Power lunges** 16 times (2 bounces on each leg, opposite hand jabs forward 2 times)
32	**Jumping jacks** (half time: 2 counts out, 2 counts in) 8 times
32	**Heel chugs** to the side (chest press with the arms) 16 times
32	**Point to the foot** 16 times
32	**Funky fish** 8 times
32	**Ophea hand jive**
32	**Power lunges** 16 times (2 bounces on each leg, opposite hand jabs forward 2 times)
32	**Jumping jacks** (half time: 2 counts out, 2 counts in) 8 times
	Throw hands up in the air on last beat

MOTION MOTION (ALLEY CAT)

Count	Cue	Instruction or pattern
Introduction		
2 of nothing	Instrumental introduction	Do nothing, wait for next counts
16	Instrumental begins	Feet together, bounce at knees
Part 1		
4		**Tap out** R 2 times (R arm punches out to side)
4		**Tap out** L 2 times (L arm punches out to side)
Part 2		
4		Push R leg out to back and back to center (both arms push out to front) 2 times
4		Push L leg out to back and back to center (both arms push out to front) 2 times
Part 3		
4		**Cross crawl** (R knee to L elbow) 2 times
4		**Cross crawl** (L knee to R elbow) 2 times

Count	Cue	Instruction or pattern
		Part 4
6		**Cross crawl** (R knee to L elbow) 2 times **Cross crawl** (L knee to R elbow) 2 times **Cross crawl** (R knee to L elbow) 2 times
2		1/4 jump turn to L (counterclockwise) and clap
		Repeat parts 1-4 until the end of the song.

MARCHING CIRCUS

Count	Cue	Instruction or pattern
16	Music starts	**March** on the spot with high knees
		Part 1
1-4		Starting with the R foot, walk backward three steps On count 4, touch L toe to the floor
5-8		Travel forward starting with the L foot and touch R toe to the floor
9-16		Repeat part 1
		Part 2
1-4		**Grapevine** R On count 4 kick L foot forward
5-8		**Grapevine** L On count 4 kick R foot forward
9-10		With a slight bend of the L knee, extend R foot forward as far as comfortably possible and tap R toe 2 times on floor
11-12		Stretch R leg back and tap toe 2 times on the floor behind
13-16		Tap R toe forward, tap R toe back, tap to R side Vigorously kick the R foot across in front of the standing leg to the L and turn body 1/4 turn to L
32		Repeat parts 1 and 2 facing side
32		Repeat parts 1 and 2 facing back
16	Music changes	**March** in place

Count	Cue	Instruction or pattern
		Part 3
1-4		Starting with the L foot, walk backward three steps On count 4, touch R toe to the floor
5-8		Travel forward starting with the R foot and touch L toe to the floor
9-16		Repeat part 3
		Part 4
1-4		**Grapevine** L On count 4 kick R foot forward
5-8		**Grapevine** R On count 4 kick L foot forward
9-10		With a slight bend of the R knee, extend L foot forward as far as comfortably possible and tap L toe 2 times on floor
11-12		Stretch L leg back and tap toe 2 times on the floor behind
13-16		Tap L toe forward, tap L toe back, tap to L side Vigorously kick the L foot across in front of the standing leg to the R and turn body 1/4 turn to R
32		Repeat parts 3 and 4 facing back
32		Repeat parts 3 and 4 facing side
6		**March** it around to the front until music ends

GRINGO (LATIN AMERICAN)

Count	Instruction or pattern
16	**March** on the spot, bending knees to the L and R; down, down, up, up 4 times, alternating toward the center
	Hands **washing windows**
32	**Shimmy shake** 4 times
16	**Grapevine** L, R 2 times (no arms, hands on waist)
16	**Grapevine** L, R 2 times (single arm circling up over head and to side)
16	**V step** (raise each arm as you step out, bring each arm in as you step back)
16	**V step** (jump forward into squat, feet apart), 2 counts Jump back (feet together), 2 counts (clap hands 2 times as you jump back)
32	**Shimmy shake** 4 times
16	**Mambo** R 4 times
16	**Mambo** L 4 times
32	**Digs** side to side, with a jump and a clap 16 times
16	**Rainbow arms** 8 times
32	**Grapevine** L, R 8 times (both arms circle upward when moving R, circle back down when moving L)
16	**Shadow boxing** 8 times (2 beats per side)
32	**Punching square** 8 times
16	**Grapevine** R, L 4 times (no arms)
16	**Grapevine** R, L 4 times (single arm circle)

Count	Instruction or pattern
32	**Grapevine** R, L 8 times (both arms circling up and down)
8	**March** on the spot, shoulder rolls back 4 times
8	**March** on the spot, shoulder rolls forward 4 times
	Punch down to the beat of the music, reach both arms up to the shoulders, then throw them in the air on the last beat—big ending

LATINIQUE

Count	Cue	Instruction or pattern
Introduction		
8		
16		**Tap out** R, L 8 times (hands at side)
16		**Tap out** and **squat** (transfer weight R, L) 8 times (hands on waist)
32		Squat diagonally forward on R foot, pressing R shoulder forward followed by L shoulder, rotating shoulders back when returning to center. Repeat to L, 4 times each side
Part 1		
32		Jog on spot (**sunrise arms**), 4 counts up, 4 counts down, 4 times
32		**Cha-cha** 8 times
16		Side lunge with **look out** R, L 2 times
16		Side **lunge** with **waves** (4 count) R, L 2 times
Part 2		
32		Punch R, L, R (in front) then step to R, slide L beside R, step to R (ending in straddle) Repeat to L. 4 times each side
32		Punch R, L, R (up), then step to R, slide L beside R, step to R (ending in straddle). Punch down R, L, R. Step to L, slide R beside L, step to L. Repeat sequence 4 times

Count	Cue	Instruction or pattern
		Part 3
32		**Shimmy shake** 4 times
32		**Shimmy shake** (**chug step** back) 4 times
		Repeat part 1
		Repeat part 2, ending with hands up

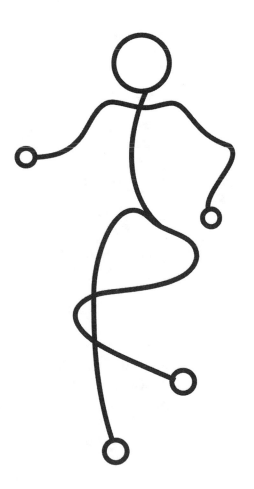

DREAM MACHINE

Count	Cue	Instruction or pattern
Part 1		
	Introduction	Bend knees and bounce
16		**Grapevine** (2 times each direction)
16		**Box steps** 4 times
8		**Tap out** R, L, R, L
4		Point R leg forward, L leg forward
4		Point R leg backward, L leg backward
4		Point R leg forward to R diagonal, L leg forward to L diagonal
4		Point R leg to back R diagonal, L leg back to L diagonal
		Repeat part 1 from **grapevine**
Part 2		
4		**Grapevine** R with turn and pull arms into body and say, "Huh" **Grapevine** L with turn and pull arms into body and say, "Huh"
4		**Grapevine** R with turn and pull arms into body and say, "Huh" **Grapevine** L with turn and pull arms into body and say, "Huh"
4		Step forward R and pivot to face back; repeat to face front; R point to R side, L point to L side

Count	Cue	Instruction or pattern
4		Step forward R and pivot to face back; repeat to face front; R point to R side, L point to L side
		Repeat part 2
Part 3		
4		**Lunge** forward with R leg for 2 counts and return to standing for 2 counts (do biceps curl at same time)
4		Repeat **lunge** with L leg
4		Repeat **lunge** R
4		Repeat **lunge** L
Part 4		
16		Turn to L and do **Tae Bo kick** sides: With hands up in boxing position, kick to side with R leg, step down, step in place 2 times, repeat with L leg, repeat
16		Repeat part 3 **lunges**
16		Repeat part 4 facing R
Part 5		
16		**Grapevine** (2 times each side)
16		**Box steps** 4 times
		Finish with arms up overhead in a V position!

Count	Instruction or pattern
16	Introduction.
16	**March** on spot.
32	**March and breathe** (4 counts up, 4 counts down).
16	**March** wide.
16	**March** wide 3 times, tap in L. Repeat sequence 3 times.
32	**Squat** (2 counts down, 2 counts up). With feet shoulder-width apart, arms reach out front and back down to hips.
32	Quarter turn to right wall, **lunge** (2 counts down, 2 counts up). Arms press out from the chest.
32	Half turn to left wall, lunge (2 counts down, 2 counts up). Arms do triceps extension.
16	Face center again. Squat (2 counts down, 2 counts up). Feet are shoulder-width apart. Arms reach out front and back down to hips 4 times.
16	**Squat** and pulse 7 times. On count 8 bring R foot in to meet L.
16	**Grapevine** 4 times.
16	**Grapevine** with gluteal kick 4 times.
8	**V step** right 2 times.
8	**V step** left 2 times.
Chorus	
8	**March** forward 4 times, tap out R, L.
8	**March** back 4 times, tap out R, L.
8	Jog forward 4 times, tap out R, L.

Count	Instruction or pattern
8	Jog back 4 times, tap out R, L.
8	**March** forward 4 times, 2 **jumping jacks**.
8	**March** back 4 times, 2 **jumping jacks**.
8	Jog forward 4 times, 2 **jumping jacks**.
8	Jog back 4 times, 2 **jumping jacks**.
	End of chorus
16	**Knee pump:** Step on R foot toward right corner and pump L knee 8 times.
16	Step touch 8 times.
16	**Knee pump:** Step on L foot toward left corner and pump R knee 8 times.
16	Step touch 8 times.
8	**Alternating knee lifts**, moving forward 4 times.
8	**Alternating knee lifts**, moving back 4 times.
16	**Power squat**: Jump out into squat position (2 counts) and jump feet together 2 times and clap 2 times. Repeat 4 times.
8	**Pulling weeds** traveling forward 4 times.
8	**Pulling weeds** traveling back 4 times.
16	**Power squat**: Jump out into squat position (2 counts) and jump feet together 2 times and clap 2 times. Repeat 4 times.
16	**Heel chugs:** Singles R, L 8 times.
16	**Heel chugs:** Doubles R, L 4 times.

(continued)

Aerobics *(continued)*

Count	Instruction or pattern
	Repeat chorus
16	**Shuffle** R (8 counts), lunge back R, L 4 times.
16	**Shuffle** L (8 counts), lunge back L, R 4 times.
16	**Step touch** 2 to the R, 2 to the L 4 times (hands on hips).
8	**Step touch** 2 to the R with R shoulder roll, 2 to the L with L shoulder roll.
8	**Step touch** 2 to the R with R arm circle, 2 to the L with L arm circle.

Count	Cue	Instruction or pattern
16	Intro music	Stand with feet shoulder-width apart.
8		4 **shoulder shrugs.**
8		**Lunge** R with full right arm circle, lunge L with full left arm circle. Repeat each side.
8		4 **shoulder shrugs.**
8		**Lunge** R with full right arm circle, lunge L with full left arm circle. Repeat each side.
16		**Squat** 2 counts down, 2 counts up. On fourth one, remain in squat position.
16		8 **torso twists** slow (2 counts each way).
16		16 **torso twists** quick.
16		8 **torso twists** slow (2 counts each way).
16		16 **torso twists** quick.
16		**Jab** R arm to L corner 4 times (2 counts out, 2 counts back).
16		**Jab** R arm to L corner 8 times (single counts).
16		**Jab** L arm to R corner 4 times (2 counts out, 2 counts back).
16		**Jab** L arm to R corner 8 times (single counts).
32		Alternating R and L **jab** (corner to corner) 2 counts out, 2 counts center 8 times.
16		Alternating R and L **jab** (corner to corner) single counts with pause in center 8 times.
16		Alternating R and L **jab** (corner to corner) 2 counts out, 2 counts center 4 times.

(continued)

Boxercise *(continued)*

Count	Cue	Instruction or pattern
32		R **knee lift** center 2 counts up, 2 counts down 8 times.
32		R **knee lift** center (single counts) 16 times.
32		L **knee lift** center 2 counts up, 2 counts down 8 times.
32		L **knee lift** center (single counts) 16 times.
32		**Boxer shuffle** 32 times.
32		L **jab** to left wall, 3 **boxer shuffles** 8 times.
32		**Boxer shuffle** 32 times.
32		R **jab** to right wall, 3 **boxer shuffles** 8 times.
16		**Speed bag** center.
16		**Speed bag** to L corner.
16		**Speed bag** to R corner.
16		**Speed bag** center.
16		**Jumping jacks** 8 times.
16		March R, L 8 times.
32		**Tae Bo kick front** R 8 times.
32		**Tae Bo kick side** R 8 times.
32		Alternating **Tae Bo kicks front and side** R 8 times.
32		**Squat** with feet together 8 times.
32		**Tae Bo kick front** L 8 times.
32		**Tae Bo kick side** L 8 times.

Count	Cue	Instruction or pattern
32		Alternating **Tae Bo kicks front and side** L 8 times.
32		**Squat** with feet together 4 times, squat with feet apart 4 times.
16		Alternating **hooks** R, L 4 times.
16		Alternating **hooks** R, L 8 times.
16		Alternating **uppercut** R, L 4 times.
16		Alternating **uppercut** R, L 8 times.
64		Repeat **hook** and **uppercut** sequence.
32		**Jumping jacks** 16 times.
32		1 **jumping jack** and 1 L **jab** to L wall, 1 **jumping jack** and 1 R **jab** to R wall 8 times.
32		**March** on spot 16 times.
32		Step together 3 times to R, 1 **cross jab** with L arm; step together 3 times to L, 1 **cross jab** with R arm. Repeat 4 times.
32		**Shuffle** R 3 counts, 1 **cross jab** L; **shuffle** L 3 counts, 1 **cross jab** R. Repeat 8 times.
16		**Step touch** 8 times.
8		**March** 4 times.
8		**March** wide 4 times.
16		**March** 8 times.
16		**March and breathe** 2 times.

Count	Cue	Instructions or pattern
16	Intro music	Step touch and clap.
Part 1		
8		**Funky V stomp:** Stomp R foot diagonally right, raising R arm straight up in direction of R leg; stomp L foot diagonally left, raising L arm straight up in direction of L leg; jog back 3 times (jogging arms) = 4 counts. V stomp to L, R, jog back 3 times = 4 counts.
8		Repeat.
8		**Kick squats:** Kick R foot forward, kick L foot forward (opposite arms reach forward and backward). Squat R with butterfly arms: Hands come together in front of chest, lift straight up when stepping out, pull elbows at 90-degree angle to sides while squatting (biceps curl). Hands come back up together and pull down in front when feet come back together. Kick L foot forward, kick R foot forward, squat L with butterfly arms.
8		Repeat.
Part 2		
8		**Funky pulling weeds:** Same as pulling weeds, but kick seat R, L, R, R, then L, R, L, L.
8		Repeat.

Count	Cue	Instructions or pattern
		Part 3
8		**Broadway cha-cha:** Dig R heel diagonally across L foot, tap R toe diagonally behind L foot to R side, and cha-cha 3 times on the spot. Dig L heel diagonally across R foot, tap L toe diagonally behind R foot to L side, and cha-cha 3 times on the spot. Arms move opposite to legs.
8		Repeat.
8		**Funky knee lifts:** Same as knee lifts, but R, L, R, R, then L, R, L, L. (Cue: single, single, double.)
8		Repeat.
8		**Funky cross crawl:** Same as cross crawl, but touch opposite elbow R, L, R, R, then L, R, L, L.
8		Repeat.
		Part 4
32	Repeat part 1	**Funky V stomp** and **kick squats.**
48	Repeat part 3	**Broadway cha-cha, funky knee lifts, funky cross crawl.**
16	Intro music	**Step touch** and clap: Walk backward 4 times, walk forward 4 times. Repeat.
16		**Funky V stomp.**
12		**Kick squats.**

LATIN MIX: CUMBIA URBANA

Count	Cue	Instructions or pattern
Part 1		
8	Music starts	**Funky Egyptian.** Same as Egyptian, but R, L, R, R and L, R, L, L (single, single, double). Repeat.
8		**Basic and side cumbia:** Dig R heel forward, touch R toe back. Arms move forward and backward opposite feet. Turn shoulders to face R and step together 2 times R, L with arm facing front, right arm facing back. **Dig** L heel forward, touch L toe back. Turn shoulders to L and step together, 2 times to L.
8		Repeat **basic and side cumbia.**
Part 2		
8	Bongo drums	**Backward crawl:** Stomp R foot forward, lift R arm straight up, and circle back around 1 time. Stomp L foot forward, lift L arm straight up, and circle back around 1 time. Stomp R foot forward 2 times, R arm straight up 1 time, and circle back around 1 time.
8		Repeat starting with L foot backward, L arm straight up, and circle back around 1 time; stomp R foot backward, R arm straight up, and circle back around 1 time; stomp L foot backward 2 times, L arm straight up 1 time; circle back around 1 time.
8		Repeat.

Count	Cue	Instructions or pattern
8	Cymbals	**Egyptian drag:** Step to R 4 times, dragging L foot with Egyptian arms. Step to L 4 times, dragging R foot with Egyptian arms.
8		Repeat.
Part 3		
8		**Circle stomp:** Turning R, stomp L foot forward 2 times, 2 times R side, 2 times back, 2 times L side. Arm action: Elbows bent, palms parallel to floor alternately pushing down (playing bongos).
8		Repeat circle stomp to L, stomp R foot forward 2 times, 2 times L side, 2 times back, 2 times R side.
8		**Single dog lifts:** Lift R leg to R side to 90-degree angle, raising extended bent arms, fingers pointing to the ground as leg rises (as if attached to a string). Lift L leg to L side to 90-degree angle, raising hands as leg rises. Repeat 4 times.
8		**Double dog lifts:** Lift R leg to R side 2 times, raising arms as leg rises. Lift L leg to L side 2 times, raising arms as leg rises. Repeat.
32	Repeat part 1	**Funky Egyptian, basic and side cumbia.**

(continued)

Count	Cue	Instructions or pattern
		Part 4
4	Bongos	**Bongo squat:** Playing bongos, squat to R side and stand up; squat to R side, stand up, and clap 1 time.
4		Playing bongos, squat to L side and stand up; squat to L side, stand up, and clap 1 time.
8		Repeat **bongo squat** and playing bongos.
8	Drums	**Backward crawl.**
32	Repeat part 3	Repeat **circle stomp** and **single dog lifts, double dog lifts.**
32	Repeat part 1	**Funky Egyptian, basic and side cumbia.**
32	Repeat part 2	Repeat **backward crawl** and **Egyptian drag.**
8		**Funky Egyptian.**

LATIN MIX: REGGAETON

Count	Cue	Instructions or pattern
8	Music starts	**Marching,** with heavy marching on beats 3, 4 and 7, 8. Arm action: alternating-arm curl-ups.
8		Repeat.
Part 1		
8	Oh, oh	**Funky hip-hop:** Step R foot to R, touch L foot beside R. Step L foot to L, touch R foot to L. Step together to R 2 times. Push arms to side in opposite direction of legs. Repeat stepping to L.
8		Repeat.
Part 2		
8	Drums	**Funky leg curls:** Standing on L foot, bend R knee and kick seat with heel 4 times while brushing R shoulder with L hand 4 times. Repeat, standing on R foot.
8		Repeat.

(continued)

Latin Mix: Reggaeton   *(continued)*

Count	Cue	Instructions or pattern
		Part 3
8	Drums	**Robot:** Step R foot diagonally to R with R foot leading 2 times with robot arms: Straight arms extended in front of body, palms facing each other, alternately moving arms up and down. Step L foot diagonally to L with L foot leading 2 times with robot arms. March backward, stepping R, L, R, L, reaching under legs each time on counts 5, 6, 7, 8. Repeat starting with L foot.
8		Repeat.
		Part 4
8	Oh, oh	**Pulsing arms:** Strong arms bent, hands clenched toward chest, pulsing action with forearms, alternating sides, moving forward 4 times and backward 4 times.
8		Repeat.
16	Drums	Repeat part 2, funky leg curls.
16	Oh, oh	Repeat part 1, funky hip-hop.
8	Oh, oh with claps	**Elbow pops:** With arms bent at 90 degrees, hands clenched close to body, lift elbows and shoulders up to R 1 time, to L 1 time, to R, and clap 2 times. Lift elbows and shoulders up to L 1 time, to R 1 time, to L 2 times, and clap 2 times.
8		Repeat.
16	Oh, oh	Repeat part 4, **pulsing arms.**
16	Oh, oh	Repeat part 2, **funky leg curls.**
16	Drums	Repeat part 3, **robot.**
16	Oh, oh	Repeat part 1, **funky hip-hop.**

LATIN MIX: LUCKY 6

Count	Cue	Instructions or pattern
12	Music starts	Clap 12 times while bouncing.
8		**Star jumps:** 2 times at half time, bringing arms to sides after each jump.
8		**Lunge** to R side with rainbow arms from R to L. Repeat to L side.
4		**Play bongos** from R to L.
8	Who! Who!	**Shoulder dig:** Step forward on R foot and dig R shoulder forward 2 times; jump up and raise the roof 2 times. Step forward on L foot and dig L shoulder forward 2 times; jump up and raise the roof 2 times.
24		Repeat 3 times. (Cue: shoulder dig on beats 1, 2 and jump up and raise the roof on beats 3, 4.)
8		**Egyptian shuffle:** Legs apart. Arm position: Start with R arm at 90-degree angle to R, palm facing up; L arm bent in front of body, parallel to floor, palm facing down, pump to R. L arm goes to 90-degree angle to L, palm facing up and R arm parallel to floor, palm facing down, pump to L. 4 times moving down, 4 times moving up.
8		Repeat.
4		**Calypso crossover:** Step L foot forward over R with pulling weeds arms; step back on R, then L. Step R foot forward over L with pulling weeds arms; step back on L, then R.
4		Repeat.

(continued)

Count	Cue	Instructions or pattern
8		**Calypso stomp:** Stomp left foot forward over right and pull horizontal arms toward chest on 1, 2 and face front and slap sides on 3, 4. Stomp R foot forward over L and pull horizontal arms toward chest on 5, 6 and face front and slap sides on 7, 8.
8		**Knee dribble:** Step R foot forward over L and dribble 1 time with R hand; step back on R foot and dribble 1 time with R hand. Step together 2 times to R and dribble 2 times with R hand. Step L foot forward over R and dribble 1 time with L hand; step back on L foot and dribble 1 time with L hand. Step together 2 times to L and dribble 2 times with L hand.
8		Repeat.
16	Who, Who	**Shoulder dig.**
16		**Egyptian shuffle.**
16		**Calypso crossover.**
8		**Jump and squat:** Jump to a squat facing R side, hands on thighs. Jump back to face front, jump to a squat facing L side, jump back to face front.
8		Repeat.
16		**Knee dribble.**
16	Who, Who	**Shoulder dig** (ends in Who, Who, Who and strike a pose).

ETHNO TENSION (AFRICAN ROUTINE)

Count	Cue	Instruction or pattern
Part 1		
16		**The giving** (4 time each side)
16		**Give more** (4 times each side)
16		**Side jump, mirror wipe** (4 times each side)
16		**The why** (4 times each side)
16		**The lion** (2 times each side)
8		**Trunk**
16		The **elephant** (4 times)
Part 2		
16		Play imaginary bongo drums rapidly from side to side and in front of body 4 counts to R, 4 counts to L, repeat 2 times
Repeat part 1		
16		**Polka step**, reach both arms up while shaking hands and fingers for 2 counts, then reach down for 2 counts; repeat 4 times
24		**Wildebeest stampede** (24 counts)
1		Jump into pose

Choreographed with inspiration from Sheela Bharath, acting vice principal of Morton Way Public School.

Count	Cue	Instruction or pattern
4		Head to chest, center and look up 4 times
4		Head side L, center, side R, center 8 times
4		**Shoulder rolls** backward
4		**Shoulder rolls** forward
8		**Side bends** (alternating arms reach up and over)
8		Both arms up: circle arms all the way around to the R
8		Both arms up: circle arms all the way around to the L
8		L leg quadriceps stretch
8		L leg extends in front on floor, foot flexed toward shin (hamstring stretch)
8		R leg quadriceps stretch
8		R leg extends in front on floor, foot flexed toward shin (hamstring stretch)
8		Feet come together Rise on toes, reach arms to ceiling
8		**Lunge** side to side 8 times
8		**Lunge** side to side 8 times Arms circle up together and down together as you **lunge**
4		Feet come together Squat down, reach arms out

Count	Cue	Instruction or pattern
8	Instrumental	Do nothing.
16	Instrumental	**Reach to the sky.** Standing tall, take one breath in and out. As you breathe in, roll shoulders up toward ears in a big circular movement, and as you breathe out, roll them back down toward hips. Do this twice.
24		Slowly raise your arms out to the sides and rotate your palms to face upward toward the sky. Keep feet together and tight. Continue to stretch arms up to the sky and bring your palms together.
	Smile it's a new day, move in a new way.	Press them together and rise up onto your toes as you are inhaling. As you begin to breathe out, start to lower your heels down to the floor, and continue to stand straight and tall with arms pointing up like an arrow. Take one full breath in and out.
16	Smile it's a new day; move in a new way. Smile it's a new day; move in a new way.	**Bow to the mountain.** Begin to separate your palms, and begin to fold your body by bending at the hips. Keep your spine straight as you exhale and bring your arms down beside your legs. Your feet do not move, and your head hangs with neck and shoulders relaxed. Bend your knees and press your abdomen to your thighs. Place your hands flat on the floor beside your feet. You will be gently tucked in a standing forward bend.

(continued)

Count	Cue	Instruction or pattern
32	I'm climbin', gonna keep on smilin', that sun is gonna keep on shinin'. I'm climbin', gonna keep on smilin', that sun is gonna keep on shinin'.	Change to **monkey.** As both knees are bent, begin to slide your left foot behind you, using your hands on the floor for support. Slide L leg back until you are in a lunge position. Turn your L foot so that your toes are pointing away from you and you feel a stretch at the top of your foot. Begin to lift your chin up, and bring your shoulders back. At this point, start to raise your hands off the floor and bring your arms in front of you, and then continue the flow to bring them above your head with palms together. As you breathe in, look up at your hands, being cautious not to tilt your head too far back. As you exhale, begin to bring the leg back in so that you are at the starting position once again.
32	Smile it's a new day, move in a new way. Smile it's a new day, move in a new way.	Repeat change to **monkey** with R leg back.
16	I'm climbin', gonna keep on smilin', that sun is gonna keep on shinin'. I'm climbin' gonna keep on smilin', that sun is gonna keep on shinin'.	**Bow to the mountain** in reverse, finishing in standing.

Count	Cue	Instruction or pattern
16	Smile it's a new day, move in a new way. Smile it's a new day, move in a new way. I'm climbin' gonna keep on smilin', that sun is gonna keep on shinin'. I'm climbin' gonna keep on smilin', that sun is gonna keep on shinin'. Smile it's a new day, move in a new way. Smile it's a new day, move in a new way.	**Dancer's pose.** While standing, keep shoulders and hips in line facing forward. Inhale and slowly raise R foot behind you, clasping your ankle with your R hand for support. Keep knees, hips, and shoulders square, and raise your L arm in front of you. Continue to raise left arm up to align with the spine. As you exhale, continue to look straight ahead and lower your arm. Let go of the R foot, and allow the foot to come to the ground. You will now be in a standing position once again. Repeat with L leg and R arm.
16	Instrumental	**Starfish.** Stand with your body in a wide T shape, with feet parallel to each other and arms stretched out to the sides at shoulder level. Begin to raise your arms up and over your head, and at the same time rise up onto tiptoes and inhale. Begin to exhale and bring feet down to soles and arms back down to shoulder height. Begin to bend forward from the hips, and gently lower your head so you can look at the ground. As you finish breathing out, place both hands on the floor in front of you between your feet. Bend the knees slightly. Relax your neck so you can drop your head right down, and inhale and exhale.

(continued)

Count	Cue	Instruction or pattern
16	Instrumental	**Windmill twist.** While in the ending pose for starfish, leave L hand between both feet so that it forms the third point in an equilateral triangle with your feet. Slowly raise R arm out to the side, and turn your head to watch your arm go straight up behind you. Take three breaths in this twist position. As the R arm comes back down, you will anchor it to the floor. Repeat the twist with the L arm moving back up toward the sky.
8	Instrumental	**Reach to the sky.**

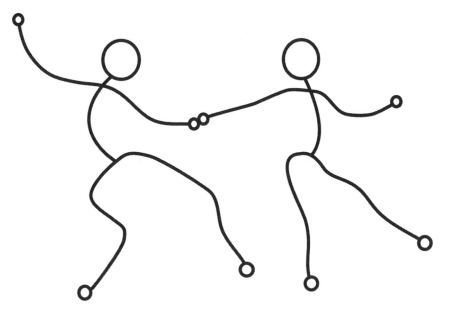

CHAPTER 9

Routines for Accessible Music

There is an abundance of catchy music available from a variety of sources. Find out what appeals to your students to keep them motivated. Cue sheets are provided on the DVD-ROM for most of these routines, and they can be transposed onto poster boards so that the participants know which funky move is coming up next. (Note that we have not provided cue sheets for "Bring It All Back" or "Agadoo" because most of the moves are prompted by words in the song.) Included in this chapter are some routines to popular music which can easily be purchased or downloaded. Give them a try and enjoy. Three songs that work really well as a warm-up include "Get Ready for This," "Bring It All Back," and "Reach."

Routine Finder

Song Title	Page number
Get Ready for This	169
Hey Baby	172
Bring It All Back	174
Reach	177
Hampsterdance	180
Popcorn	182
Cotton-Eyed Joe	184
Dance to the Music	185
Kokomo	186
Agadoo	188
Lollipop	190
Up	192
Chicken Dance	193
Follow the Leader	194
Rock Around the Clock	196
Move This	197
Havin' a Party	198
I Will Survive	200
We Like to Party	202

GET READY FOR THIS

Count	Cue	Instruction or pattern
Part 1		
2		Slap knees with hands 2 times
2		Clap hands 2 times
2		Palms down, pass R hand over L 2 times
2		Palms down, pass L hand over R 2 times
2		Strike R fist on top of L fist 2 times
2		Strike L fist on top of R fist 2 times
2		Touch R elbow with L fist 2 times
2		Touch L elbow with R fist 2 times
4		Swim (front crawl) with L arm
4		Swim (front crawl) with R arm
4		Swim (back crawl) with L arm
4		Swim (back crawl) with R arm
End part 1		
	Y'all ready for this?	Point both fingers away from body
		Repeat part 1
Part 2		
8		Swim with both arms (breaststroke) 2 times

(continued)

Get Ready for This *(continued)*

Count	Cue	Instruction or pattern
4		**Lasso** with R hand
4		**Lasso** with L hand
4		**Hitchhike** with R thumb
4		**Hitchhike** with L thumb
2		Reach up with R hand and catch an imaginary fly
2		Place the fly in the palm of your L hand
2		Slap the fly with R hand
2		Blow the fly off your palm
		Repeat part 1
64	Bing, bing, bing	**Ophea hand jive** 2 times
	Y'all ready for this?	Point both fingers away from body
64		**Ophea hand jive** 2 times
	Y'all ready for this?	Point both fingers away from body
		Repeat part 1
Part 3		
3		**Roll it** (hands in front)
1		Punch R hand
3		**Roll it**
1		Punch L hand
3		**Roll it**

Count	Cue	Instruction or pattern
1		Punch R hand
2		**Roll it**
2		Punch R hand, then L hand
		Repeat part 3
		Repeat parts 1 and 2
4		Clap 4 times (with last clap make it look as if you're hitting cymbals, and slowly separate hands)

Music from Crazy Frog Presents Crazy Hits

HEY BABY

This routine is great for audience participation. Divide assembly or group into two parts. One side is the "oooh" group, and the other is the "ahhh" group. (In a class, you can have the girls be the "ooohs" and the boys the "ahhhs.") The leader points to the corresponding group during the song.

Count	Cue	Instruction or pattern
16	Introduction	**Attitude**
Part 1		
10	Hey baby	**Roll it**
2	Oooh	Point to group 1
2	Ahhh	Point to group 2
14	I want to know if you'll be my girl	**Roll it** (other way)
4	Uno, dos, tres, cuatro	Hold up fingers for each count to four
		Repeat part 1
32	Instrumental	**Digs** with clap 16 times
32	When I saw you walking down the street	**Disco** 4 times each side Repeat
Repeat part 1		
32		**Funky fish** 8 times
8	When you turn and walk away	**Monkeys** up and down 4 times
8	That's when I wanna say	**Monkeys** to the R 4 times

Count	Cue	Instruction or pattern
8	C'mon baby give me a whirl	**Monkeys** to the L 4 times
8	I wanna know, I wanna know oh, oh	**Monkeys** up and down 4 times
16	When you turn and walk away . . .	**Waves** 8 times (alternating arms every 2 beats)
16	C'mon baby give me a whirl	**Hit the table** 4 times
Repeat part 1		
	Instrumental end Ta ta tee-tee ta	Punch arms down with beat

Music from Crazy Frog Presents Crazy Hits

BRING IT ALL BACK

NOTES: The lyrics are very positive, and most of the motions go with the words.

Count	Cue	Instruction or pattern
		Clap through the introduction
Part 1		
	Don't	R hand up at shoulder, palm out
	stop	Push hand straight out in front
	never	Point both fingers up, near shoulders
	give up	Raise pointed fingers above head
	Hold your head high	Palms facing down, fingers tap under chin
	and reach the top	**Raise the roof**
	Let the world see what you have got	**Hey you**
	Bring it all back to	**Roll it** (backward)
	you	Point forward with your fingers, thumbs up
Part 2		
	Hold on to what you try to be	Clap knees with both hands 2 times
		Clap hands 2 times
		Palms down, pass R hand over L 2 times

Count	Cue	Instruction or pattern
		Palms down, pass L hand over R 2 times
		Strike R fist on top of L fist 2 times
		Strike L fist on top of R fist 2 times*
		R thumb up, pointing over R shoulder
		L thumb up, pointing over L shoulder
		Repeat part 2, 3 times until * (around "so don't you stop tryin'!")
	*. . . around, so don't you stop tryin'!	Point finger and make circles over your head; if standing, turn around
		Repeat part 1
Part 3		
	Dream of	Palms together by side of face, as if you are sleeping
	falling in love	Hands clasped together over heart
	Anything you've been thinking of	Tap finger at temple
	When the world seems to	Bring one fist, then the other, up below chin
	get too tough	**Punch** it out 3 times
	Bring it all back to	**Roll it** (backward)
	you	Point forward with fingers, thumbs up

(continued)

Count	Cue	Instruction or pattern
Part 4		
16	Nah, nah, nah	**Digs** 4 times each direction
		Repeat part 2, 3 times, last one with *so don't you stop tryin'!
32	Try not to worry 'bout a thing	Repeat part 1, part 3, part 1, part 4 2 times, part 1 2 times
		Repeat part 1, part 3, part 1, part 3, part 1, part 3, part 1

Music by S Club 7. Choreographed by Joan Erickson, music teacher at Morton Way Public School.

REACH

Count	Cue	Instruction or pattern
Introduction		Clap through introduction
Part 1		
16	When the world	**Hit the table** 4 times
16	When it seems, all your hopes	**Waves** (2 counts per wave) 8 times
1	We've got to all stick together	*Push your R hand out, palm facing forward (like "stop")*
1		*Push your L hand out beside your R hand*
1		*Push your R hand up over your head, palm facing the roof*
1		*Push your L hand up, beside your R*
		Repeat *italicized pattern* 3x
2	I've got	Point thumbs at yourself 2 times
4	you and you've got	Point fingers away from yourself 4 times
2	me so	Point thumbs at yourself 2 times
Part 2		
1	Reach	Reach up with your R hand over your head, palm out, and bring it down
1	for the	Reach up with your L hand over your head, palm out, and bring it down
2	stars	Reach up with both hands, spread fingers apart, bring them down and repeat

(continued)

Reach *(continued)*

Count	Cue	Instruction or pattern
2	Climb every	Hands in front, fingers bent as if climbing (move them up)
2	mountain higher	Swoop both hands down in front (as if they're going down a mountain)
1	Reach for the stars	Reach hands up (R, L, and both as done earlier for "reach for the stars")
1	Follow your	Point with your R hand across body
2	heart's desire	Bring hand together with other hand in front of heart (thump chest 2 times)
4	Reach for the stars	Reach hands up (R, L, and both as done earlier for "reach for the stars")
8	And when that rainbow's	**Rainbow arms** 1 time
4	That's when your dreams	With both hands indicate clouds (dreams) around head
8	True	"Rock" or **wave** hands back and forth above head, to the beat
	There's a place	Repeat parts 1 and 2
Part 3		
3	Don't believe in all that	Shake your finger
1	you've been	Point with both fingers
1	told	Hold hands up to mouth
	The sky's the limit	Point up
	you can reach your	Reach upward with R hand
	goal	Both arms straight up, palms facing in, as if signaling a touchdown in football

Count	Cue	Instruction or pattern
	No one knows just what the	Arms out, shrug your shoulders
	future	Stretch arms out in front
	holds	Curl arms back to chest, as if you're holding something close
	There ain't nothing you can't be	Shake your finger
	There's a whole world	Make your arms into a big circle over your head
	at your feet	Bend at the waist so the circle ("the world") is now at your feet
	I said reach	Reach with both arms above head
	Climb every	Climbing action with hands moving up
	mountain	Swoop your arms down in front
	(Reach)	Reach with both arms above your head
	Reach for the moon	Curl both arms around your head like a crescent moon
	(Reach)	Reach with both arms above your head
	Follow that rainbow	R arm starts on L side of the body and slowly arcs across to R side, like a rainbow
	and your dreams will all come true	With both hands indicate clouds (dreams) around head
		Repeat part 2 until the end of the song

Artist: S Club 7. Choreographed by Joan Erickson, music teacher at Morton Way Public School.

HAMPSTERDANCE

Count	Cue	Instruction or pattern
16	Introduction	Jump in place, pumping arms forward and back together in time to the music (16 times)
2		Pause
16		**Heel chugs** with arm press forward (8 times)
Part 1		
	Yeee haw!	Pause (call out, "Yeee haw!")
	i) Here we go! ii) Let's try it!	Point index finger to the ceiling then point forward, thumbs up
32		**Grapevine** R, L with jump and clap 4 times
	i) That's it! ii) You're catching on!	Point both index fingers forward, thumbs up
32		Walk and clap 4 times
	i) That's all there is to it! ii)Yeee haw! Terrific!	Point both index fingers forward, thumbs up (second time through, call out, "Yeee haw!" at the same time as you point)
16		**Jumping jacks** 8 times
16		Singles (half jumping jacks—R heel forward, R arm up; L heel forward, L arm up) 8 times
16		**Waves** 8 times
16		**Hit the table** 4 times

Count	Cue	Instruction or pattern
		Part 2
16	Alright everybody now here we go	**Clapping square** 4 times
8	Bounce in time	Bounces (or jumps) 8 times
4	Just shake your thing	Shake shoulders and arms
4	Now spin around	Spin 360 degrees on the spot
		Repeat part 1
8	C'mon everybody	**Clapping square** 8 times
8		Hop on L foot, pumping arms forward and back together in time to the music
8		Hop on R foot, pumping arms forward and back together in time to the music
16		Repeat above 2 steps
16		**Heel chugs** with arm press forward 8 times
16		Jog in place
16		**March** in place with vigor
16		**March** in place lightly
	Laughing	Shake shoulders as you touch the ground

POPCORN

Count	Cue	Instruction or pattern
		Part 1
16	Introduction	Squat down low, balancing on balls of feet and hands on floor.
16		Bounce gently in this position by lifting hips slightly, leaving hands on floor.
16		Pop up into standing straddle with knees bent and hands on knees. Repeatedly press shoulders forward L, R, L, R.
16		Pop up to standing position. Jump up and down while pumping arms together forward and backward.
16		Jump and wave both arms overhead.
		Repeat part 1.
		Part 2
32	Bawk, bawk, chicky, chicky	**Monkeys**, hamstring curls 16 times
8		Face R. Step to R on R, while pressing arms out from R shoulder. Slide L to meet R, bringing arms in. Repeat 4 times. Clap and pivot to L.
8		Swivel to L. Step to L on L, while pressing arms out from L shoulder. Slide R to meet L, bringing arms in. Repeat 4 times. Clap and pivot.
8		Repeat sequence 4 times to R.
8		Repeat sequence 4 times to L.

Count	Cue	Instruction or pattern
		Repeat part 1.
		Repeat part 2.
		Repeat part 1.
4	Finale	Slowly lower arms to sides from overhead.

Music from Crazy Frog Presents Crazy Hits

COTTON-EYED JOE

Counts	Instruction or pattern
32	2 kicks on R, feet together R, L, R, 2 kicks on L, feet together L, R, L 8 times
32	Squat side to side (2 counts each side) 8 times
16	**Grapevine** R to L 4 times
16	**Shuffle step** 4 counts R, 4 counts L 4 times
32	**Jumping jacks** 16 times
32	2 kicks on R, feet together R, L, R, 2 kicks on L, feet together L, R, L 8 times
16	**Grapevine** R to L 4 times
16	**Shuffle step** 4 counts R, 4 counts L 4 times
16	Jog on the spot (no arms), single counts 16 times
16	Jog on the spot 2 counts each leg (arms up 2, down 2) 8 times
32	**Heel chugs** (arms push out away from chest) 16 times
32	2 kicks on R, feet together R, L, R, 2 kicks on L, feet together L, R, L 8 times
16	**Grapevine** R to L 4 times
16	**Shuffle step** 4 counts R, 4 counts L 4 times
16	March feet in and out 16 times
16	**March** on the spot 16 times
16	2 kicks on R, feet together R, L, R, 2 kicks on L, feet together L, R, L 4 times

Music from Crazy Frog Presents Crazy Hits

DANCE TO THE MUSIC

Counts	Cue	Instruction or pattern
32		Step touch side to side, clap hands 16 times
16	Boom, boom	**Attitude** 2 times
32	Dance to the music	**Heel digs** 16 times
16	All we need	**Pulling weeds** 8 times
16	"Drums"	**Monkeys** with hamstring curls
16	I'm going to add	**Hey you** 4 times
16	"Guitar"	**Squish the bug** 8 times
16	I'm going to add	**Tap out**, alternating arms up and over 8 times
16	"Bass"	**Tap out, raise the roof** 8 times
16	You might like	**V step** (step out, out, in, in) 4 times
16	"Organ"	**Hitchhike** 8 times
16	If I could hear	**Twisty jumps** to the R 8 times, L 8 times
16	"Instrumental"	**Cross crawl** 8 times
48	Listen to me	**Funky fish** 4 times **Hit the table** 4 times **Punching down** 4 times
32	Boom, boom	Knees together, little bounces, **roll it**, arms (R, L)
	Dance to the music	**Step touch** side to side, clap hands (until the end)

Artist: Sly and the Family Stone

Count	Cue	Instruction or pattern
	Music	Pulse and snap fingers 4 times
24	Aruba	**Ophea hand jive:** Pull R elbow down 2 times Push R elbow out to side 2 times Roll hand in front Wave R arm Repeat sequence with L arm Repeat sequence with both arms
	Jamaica	Sway R, then L
Part 1		
64	Off the Florida Keys	**Grapevine** R, L Walk forward, R, L, R, and hop Walk backward, R, L, R, and hop Repeat sequence 4 times
Part 2		
32	Aruba	**Ophea hand jive**
8	Take it slow	Jump forward, rolling arms Jump backward, rolling arms Repeat sequence
8	We want to go	Hit L hip with R hand Hit R hip with L hand Hit R seat with R hand Hit L seat with L hand Jump forward, backward, forward, clap
Part 3		
8	Martinique	Step to R 2 times, Step L 2 times Clap on counts 2, 4, 6, 8 (digging arms)

Count	Cue	Instruction or pattern
	Moving out to sea	Repeat parts 1, 2, and 3
		Repeat parts 1 and 2 Repeat part 3 until the music ends

Artist: Beach Boys. Adapted from OPHEA, but can use any upbeat music.

AGADOO

Count	Cue	Instruction or pattern
	Aga	Hold two fingers up on each hand
	doo-do-do	Push fingers forward 3x
	Push pineapple	Push both hands out with palms out 2 times
	Shake the tree	Clasp hands and swing an arc from your L shoulder, out in front of your body to your R shoulder and back to your L
		Repeat motions agadoo-do-do and push pineapple
	Grind coffee	Roll fists and bend forward at the waist
	To the L	Clap hands and reach L
	To the R	Clap hands and reach R
	Jump up	Pat your knees, then jump (if you're standing), raising your hands over your head
	and down	Pat your knees
	and to the knees	Cross and uncross your hands as you pat your knees
	Come and dance	Clap the rhythm

Count	Cue	Instruction or pattern
		If standing during the verse portion of the agadoo, use **grapevine** with a kick; if seated, you can roll your fists in big circles or tap your fingers in the air across your body and fling your fingers back over your L shoulder, then repeat to your R (the children enjoy it when they can call out "Woo" when they fling).
		At the end of the song, toss both hands up, fling your fingers back over your shoulders, and let out a "Woo."

Artist: Black Lace

LOLLIPOP

Count	Cue	Instruction or pattern
Part 1		
		Clap to music
8	Lollipop, Lollipop	R hand up R hand out R hand down R hand out
8		Repeat with L hand
8		Repeat with both hands
	Pop!	Jump up
	B-boom, boom, boom	Make Pac-Man chomps with your hands to the beat while slowly bending knees
	Lollipop, Lollipop	Repeat part 1
Part 2: verse		
32	You're my baby Lollipop	**Grapevine** L, R 4 times
	Start on: I called him Lollipop	Repeat part 1
Part 3: verse		
8	Sweeter than candy	Twist, normal
8		Twist, standing on R foot
8		Twist, standing on L foot
8		Twist, as low as you can go
	Lollipop, Lollipop	Repeat part 1

Count	Cue	Instruction or pattern
Part 4: verse		
32	The crazy way	Backward strut, 4 steps Forward strut, 4 steps Repeat sequence 4 times
	I called him Lollipop	Repeat part 1 2 times
		Finish with a pose!

Artist: the Chordettes. Adapted, by permission, from L. Potapczyk, *Dances even I would do* (Ontario: CIRA).

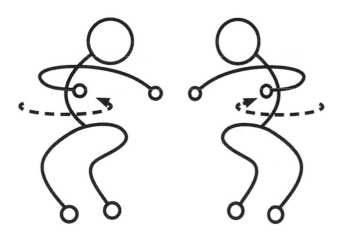

Count	Cue	Instruction or pattern
	Music starts	**Raise the roof** and **tap out**
32	It's 'bout	**Heel digs**, chest press (to the front) 16 times
32	Even my skin	**Cross crawl** 16 times
32	Up, up, up	Jump 4 times, **march** 4 times (4 times)
32	Even something	**Pulling weeds** 16 times
32	Up, up, up	Jump 4 times, **march** 4 times (4 times)
32	Oh yeah, yeah	**Side touch** and swing 16 times
32	When everything is	Arm circles backward 8 times, forward 8 times
32	It's 'bout	**Heel digs**, chest press 16 times
32	Up, up, up	**Jump** 4 times, **march** 4 times (4 times)
32	Oh I'm going up	**Lunge** side to side (no arms) 16 times
16	Yeah, yeah, yeah	**Lunge** side to side, turn wrists over 8 times

Artist: Shania Twain

CHICKEN DANCE

Count	Cue	Instruction or pattern
4		Hold hands up in front and pinch your fingers and thumbs together; "chirp" your fingers together 4 times
4		With your arms in wing position (hands tucked in armpits), flap wings 4 times
4		Wiggle your tail feathers down to the floor 4 times
4		Clap your hands 4 times
		Repeat sequence 3 times to complete the chorus
8		**Jumping jacks** 4 times
8		**Waves** 4 times
8		**Power lunge** with punch 2 times on each leg
8		**March** in place with high knees while pumping the arms 8 times
		Repeat entire sequence until song ends

This is more fun if you use the version of "Chicken Dance" that speeds up with every verse.

FOLLOW THE LEADER

Count	Cue	Instruction or pattern
32	Follow the leader (**chorus**)	3 steps to R (shaking hands at waist), 3 quick claps, 3 steps to L (shaking hands at waist), 3 quick claps
16	Hands up, hands down	Wave hands up and shake hands down at waist with beat
48	One hand in the air	Wave one hand L to R slowly, then double time
32	Follow the leader	Repeat **chorus**
32	Jump to the left	With feet together, jump to L (2 claps), jump to R (2 claps)
32	Clap and wave	4 claps in front of body (low), wave high for 4
32	Follow the leader	Repeat **chorus**
16	Now repeat after me	**Step touch** side to side (arms clap overhead as feet come together)
32	I love Soca	Walk up for 4 (arms move up toward ceiling as you walk up), walk back for 4 (arms come back down to sides)
8	Everybody scream	Jump into a star position and *scream!*
32	Follow the leader	Repeat **chorus**
16	On four	Step touch side to side (arms clap overhead as feet come together)
16	One	Feet wide apart, R arm points diagonally to R corner for 4 counts, to L for 4, R for 2, L for 2, R, L, R, L (singles)
16	Jump and wave	Jump and wave hands in the air; can jump around in a circle on repeats

Count	Cue	Instruction or pattern
24	The roof	L leg crosses over R and turn a complete circle; ski jump to R on "burn" and L on "burn"
32	Follow the leader	Repeat **chorus**
48	Now when I count to four	Step touch side to side (arms clap overhead as feet come together)
16	One ... two ... three	Feet wide apart, R arm points diagonally to R corner for 4 counts, to L for 4, R for 2, L for 2, R, L, R, L (singles)
32	Move it to the left	Facing R wall, take tiny steps while wiggling shoulder and hips, repeat to the L
32	Central ... jump and wave	Jump and wave hands in the air; can jump around in a circle on repeats
32	Follow the leader	Repeat **chorus**

Artist: The Soca Boys. This song has been around for a couple of years now. Many students will know their own version of this dance. In this English version of the song, the lyrics provide the best instructions.

ROCK AROUND THE CLOCK

Count	Cue	Instruction or pattern
Introduction 16		**Dig** and clap hands 16 times
Verse 16	Put your glad rags on	**Swivels** R, L 16 times
8		**Monkeys** 8 times
Verse 24	When the clock strikes 2	**Heel digs** to the side; push away with arms 24 times
24	Instrumental	**Skip in place** (swing arms as if turning a rope) 24 times
Verse 24	When the chimes ring 5	**Charleston** (step forward on R foot, point L foot out in front, step back on L foot, point R foot back) 6 times
Verse 24	When it's 8, 9, 10	**Alternating leg kicks** (move around in a circle) 24 times
24	Instrumental	**Box step** (step forward on R foot, cross L foot over and step in front of R, step back on L foot) 6 times
Verse 24	When the clock strikes 12	**Walk and clap** forward, backward 8 times **Grapevine** R, L **Walk and clap** forward, backward 8 times
End	Instrumental	**Sink**

Artist: Bill Haley and the Comets

MOVE THIS

Count	Cue	Instruction or pattern
32		**Roll it** 4 times each direction
32	Shake that body	**Shimmy shake** 4 times
32	People don't you know	**Grapevine** R, L 4 times
32	Baby let me show you how to do this	**Walk and clap** 4 times
32	People don't you know	**Hit the table** 8 times
32	Baby let me show you how to do this (until "shake that body for me")	**Dig** with clap 16 times
16		**Shimmy shake** 2 times
32	People don't you know	**Grapevine** R, L 4 times
32		**Wave** 16 times
32	Baby let me show you how to do this	**Power lunge**, with punch 16 times
32	Instrumental	**Funky fish** 8 times
64	Shake that body	**Disco** 8 times each side
32	You've gotta move this	**Pulling weeds** 16 times
32	Baby let me show you how to do this	**Funky chicken** 32 times
32	People don't you know	**Grapevine** R, L 4 times
32	Toes be tapping, fingers snapping	**Shaker fists** R, L 16 times
		Clap to the end

Artist: Technotronic. This routine demonstrates some of the numerous moves you can use with an upbeat song. It is easy to substitute your favorite move for any of these. The routine is easy to follow because most of the moves are repeated for 32 beats.

HAVIN' A PARTY

Count	Cue	Instruction or pattern
8		8 counts in
16	Oh come on	**Tap out** wide, swing arms L to R
16	Wow!	Drop arms, **shoulder shrugs** 8 times
16	I'm havin' me a party	**Cross crawl** to the back 8 times
16	This ain't just	**Cross crawl** to the front 8 times
16	It's gonna be really really hot	**Cross crawl** to the back (add hop) 8 times
16	Lots of one on one	**Cross crawl** to the front (add hop) 8 times
14	It doesn't matter	**Crisscross jumps**
2	There	Crouch down (touch floor) and jump to the ceiling on "Wow"
Chorus		
4	I'm havin' a party	**Shimmy shake**
4		Hop back and clap (4 times)
4	A party for two	Roll hands and walk forward (4 times)
4		Hop back and clap (4 times)
16		**Repeat chorus: shimmy shake**
16	You'll be sexy	**Tap out**, punch front (R, L) 8 times
16	I'm gonna do	**Tap out**, punch up (R, L) 8 times
14	It doesn't matter	Quick **lunges** front to back, **punch it out**

Count	Cue	Instruction or pattern
2	There	Crouch down (touch floor) and jump to the ceiling on "Wow"
32		**Repeat chorus: shimmy shake**
8	I'm here	R foot planted, tap L foot around in a full circle
8	We're gonna party	L foot planted, tap R foot around in a full circle
16	Don't think about it	2 jumps forward (arms punch to ceiling), 2 jumps back (2 claps)
32		**Jumping jacks**
16	It doesn't matter	**Power lunges** (R, L) 8 times (2 counts each side)
32		**Repeat Chorus: shimmy shake**
32	Party	Jog on spot
16	Come on	**March** on spot
16		**Heel digs** to the front (with biceps curls)

Artist: Shania Twain

Count	Cue	Instruction or pattern
16	First I was afraid	**March and breathe** (arms out and up 4 counts, shake/flick them down for 4, to the beat) 4 times
4	Dey, dey, dey, dey	Alternating **shoulder shrugs** 2 times
Part 1		
16	And so you're back (And you see me)	**March** 16 times
16	I should've changed (And so you felt like)	**Knees up** (marching) 16 times
8	Alright now go!	**Grapevine** R, L
8	Just turn around now	**Grapevine with turn** R, L
16	Weren't you the one	**Grapevine** R, L 2 times
32	Oh no, not I	**Walk and clap** 4 times
	Pause, on second verse only	Clap hands
28	Chorus: La, la, la	**Jumping jacks** 14 times
4	Dey, dey, dey, dey	Alternating **shoulder shrugs** 2 times
28	Bing, bing, bing	**Alternating knee lifts** 14 times
	Dey, dey, dey, dey	Alternating **shoulder shrugs** 2 times
Part 1 ends		

Count	Cue	Instruction or pattern
32	It took all the strength I had	**Power lunge** with punch 16 times
		Repeat part 1
28	Bing, bing, bing	**Wave** 14 times, alternating arms every 2 beats
4	Dey, dey, dey, dey	Alternating **shoulder shrugs**

From Crazy Frog Presents More Crazy Hits

WE LIKE TO PARTY

Count	Cue	Instruction or pattern
Introduction		
16	The crazy frog is coming (4 times)	Jump and wave.
Part 1		
4	The crazy frog is coming	Arms out in front, palms up, curl fingers toward self 4 times.
4	And everybody's jumping	Jump up and down. Pointer fingers point up while hands bounce up and down in sync with the jumping 4 times.
4	New York and San Francisco	Arms in front with palms facing each other. Alternately bend elbows to bring hand toward head 4 times (represents streets).
4	And inter-city disco	Disco 2 times.*
4	The wheels are still a-turning	Bend down into squat while fists rotate like a choo-choo; return to standing.
4	And traffic lights are burning	With palms out, sway hands in front of body while bending knees into a squat, then return to standing.
4	So if you like to party	Turn sideways and bounce pointer finger 4 times, moving hips.*
4	Get on and move your body	Shake fists while turning 360 degrees.
End of part 1		
32	We like to party	**Grapevine** R, L 4 times.
4	I've got something to	Point thumbs toward chest, bouncing hands 4 times.

Count	Cue	Instruction or pattern
4	tell ya	Straighten arms, pointing both fingers away, bouncing hands 4 times.
4	I've got news for	Point thumbs toward chest, bouncing hands 4 times.
4	you	Straighten arms, pointing both fingers away, bouncing hands 4 times.
8	Gonna put some wheels in motion	**Roll it,** down and up.
2	Get ready	R arm straight out, palm down.
2	'cause we're	L arm straight out, palm down.
4	comin' through	**Breaststroke.**
	Part 2	
	(Pause in words)	Make fists and bend arms so fists are at shoulder level.
2	Hey now	Punch R fist up, return to shoulder.
2	Hey now	Punch L fist up, return to shoulder.
2	Hear's what I	Pause, standing still with fists at shoulder level.
2	say now	Punch both fists up, return to shoulder.
2	Happi-	R arm straight out, palm down.
2	ness is	L arm straight out, palm down.
4	just around the corner	**Breaststroke.**
2	Hey now	Punch R fist up, return to shoulder.
2	Hey now	Punch L fist up, return to shoulder.

(continued)

We Like to Party *(continued)*

Count	Cue	Instruction or pattern
2	Hear's what I	Pause, standing still with fists at shoulder level.
2	say now	Punch both fists up, return to shoulder.
4	We'll be there for	Point thumbs toward chest, bouncing hands 4 times.
2	you	Straighten arms, pointing both fingers away.
End of part 2		
64		Repeat part 1 (2 times)
32	We like to party…	**Grapevine** R, L 4 times.
32		Repeat part 2
96		Repeat part 1 (3 times)
16	The crazy frog is comin'	Jump and wave.
64		Repeat part 1 (2 times)
4	The crazy frog is comin'	Finale.

*When part is repeated, switch sides for disco and pointing or turning so both sides of the body are used.

Music from Crazy Frog Presents Crazy Hits. Choreographed by Manju Lota, teacher, Morton Way P.S.

PART IV

GET EVERYBODY ON BOARD!
Gaining Program Support and Assessing Your Program

As a DPA champion, you know that daily physical activity is an enjoyable way for children to improve their health and learn at school. You will need others to support and contribute to your program for continued success. Chapter 10 describes how to communicate the DPA goals and how to find support for your program. We also include some ideas on how to solve some common challenges of DPA.

An important aspect of school programs is assessing the effectiveness of meeting goals. Chapter 11 provides ways and means of conducting school-wide assessments, teacher assessments, and participant assessments. Without evaluating, you cannot be sure you have been successful. Once implemented, a successful DPA program is something to celebrate. Assessment allows the opportunity for improvement and, of course, gives reasons for celebration.

CHAPTER 10

Supporting Your DPA Program

An effective DPA program requires initial and ongoing support. Communicating the goals of the DPA program is an excellent starting point. Administrators (particularly the principal), school staff, students, parents, and the community can become pillars of support for DPA. Financial support is always required for purchasing equipment and resources. Celebrating the success of the program can also encourage support. There are also many incentive programs and Web-based resources to encourage, equip, and support your DPA program.

COMMUNICATING PROGRAM GOALS

The goal of a daily physical activity program is to increase activity levels in order to help prevent obesity and disease in children and youth. In many cases, daily physical activity cannot always be accomplished during physical education class. Inform your school administrators about what daily physical activity is and why it is an important part of schools, curriculum, and healthy living.

The following are ideas for making information available to staff, students, parents, and the community:

- Create a bulletin board in a visible area of the school with information on DPA as well as ideas for adding physical activity and making healthy lifestyle choices.
- Involve the local media by providing updates of events that are going on in your school as they relate to DPA.
- Run events throughout the entire school, and invite parents and the community to become involved.
- Provide in-service training to help staff better understand how to lead DPA and also see its importance in schools.
- Create awards for people who are working hard at DPA.
- Create a DPA calendar to be included in the regular school calendar or newsletters.
- Promote the good things you are doing using school newsletters, community newsletters, posters, announcements, community newspapers, Web sites, and, of course, word of mouth.

Use the facts and statistics in chapter 1 to communicate the need for DPA and its tremendous benefits. In addition to posting information in the school newsletter, promote DPA through a separate newsletter. We have created a sample DPA newsletter for you (see appendix B). DPA newsletters can be sent out at the beginning of a school year and on a regular schedule throughout the year.

PILLARS FOR YOUR PROGRAM

Every program needs pillars of support. Initially you will need the support of the school administration to begin the program. You will also need the continuing support of administration and the school staff. Student support, enthusiasm, and motivation for your program are important as well. When parents and community members support the DPA program, the job of the leaders is much easier. Financial support is also needed for equipment, resources, and celebrations. We have a few ideas for soliciting from each of these areas of support.

Administrative Support

Administrative support includes administrators at the school district and school board level. Look for an advocate at all the administrative levels, and communicate often about your program. Take students to the Board of Education meetings or trustee meetings.

School Support

Some schools are challenged to find support for DPA from the principal and vice principal. The most important role for school principals is to provide the support necessary to ensure a quality daily physical activity program. Principals can be involved in planning, implementing, monitoring, and reviewing their schools' DPA. The first and most important step that principals can take in ensuring a quality DPA program is being a role model for staff and students. Modeling a healthy, active lifestyle will send the message to both staff and students that the principal believes in this initiative with a positive attitude and open mind. The second step is to begin to think outside the box, allowing for more ideas to be generated and a wider variety of activities to be created.

The third step is to be supportive of staff, parents, and community members who are working to create a DPA program. These people may need support with scheduling, bookings, in-service training, and consultative meetings. The principal should try to remove obstacles to ensure that everyone believes DPA is obtainable. Other support areas include ensuring that teachers have access to equipment and resources, consulting with teachers in advance about areas of concern regarding DPA, encouraging staff to provide input, providing flexibility in the school's framework for implementing the DPA (time, schedules), looking for opportunities for collaboration between teachers, and providing opportunities for mentoring by teachers who are comfortable with or experienced in various forms of physical activity.

If you are having difficulty convincing your principal about the benefits of DPA, present the facts and statistics from chapter 1 (page 6), and emphasize the impact on learning and morale. As a teacher, be sure to model daily activity in classes where the teachers are supportive. Use the success stories from these classes to support your program and any proposals for growth.

Teacher Support

To obtain teacher and staff support you may need to sell the idea. Begin by meeting with the administration so that daily physical activity is part of a school plan. Start with people who are supporters of your program, and gradually build support with others. Be patient. Let the results speak for themselves. Listen to feedback, and involve those with concerns in finding solutions.

Promote the benefits of regular physical activity, and have fun modeling, demonstrating, and sharing ideas for fitness activities at meetings. Provide write-ups of activities, tips, assistance, and reminders on an ongoing basis. Share success stories. Convince your principal to allow you to introduce a new daily physical activity at each monthly staff meeting. Some teachers will continue to feel uncomfortable, and you can help by training student leaders as well as providing workshops and ideas for teachers and leaders. Make the program as convenient as possible for the teachers. Encourage students to thank the teachers. Encourage the teachers to provide support however they are comfortable (e.g., participating, supporting the student leaders, encouraging class participation). Start simply, one thing at a time.

Student Enthusiasm

Most students will enjoy the break from seatwork and love DPA. You can work with the students to make up new activities. Include sport skills, and provide a balanced choice of activities. Ask students which activities they like and would like to do more often. Keep groups small for maximum participation. With older students, staff-versus-students challenges at lunchtimes are always popular and help to motivate participants. Some students may not think the DPA activities are very fun, but those who are the most apathetic toward DPA may become the most energetic leaders. Consider inviting disinterested students to become leaders.

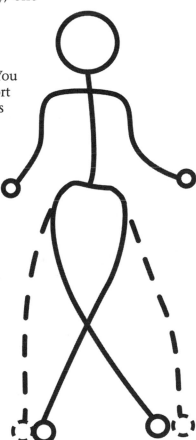

Parent Support

Parent support is crucial for meeting the DPA goals of increasing physical activity and the development of lifelong daily activity. You may need to be patient with parents who do not yet see the value of DPA. Develop a presentation for the parent council outlining the benefits, process, and connections to learning, emphasizing that academics are being enhanced, not compromised. Regularly communicate the positive aspects in the school newsletter. Get support from the health unit, and include endorsements in school publications.

Community Support

Families, schools, and communities that work together can have the biggest effect on students' lives. The community can provide leaders for schoolwide DPA, financial and equipment resources, and encouragement for everyone to move. Be sure to profile your program in local media.

Financial Support

Although some school districts provide direct financial support for DPA, other schools need to be creative in obtaining resources. Try to work with community businesses to support your program. Schools can request money from the school council. Also consider doing a school or group fund-raiser focused on physical activity, such as Jump Rope for Heart, a move-a-thon, a dance-a-thon, or Active Schools initiatives. Other suggestions include having students do presentations in the community, applying for grants (e.g., from Jump Rope for Heart), and partnering with the health unit and local recreation. Many activities can also be modified so that music and equipment are not required.

Troubleshooting Tips for DPA Challenges

Use these ideas to kick-start your thinking about common challenges. Remember that one solution may not work for all schools and situations. Keep talking and trying until you find the system that works for you. It will be worth the effort.

- Look for an advocate on the school board and in the school district.
- Bring some students to a school board meeting, or invite board members to observe DPA at your school.
- Emphasize the impact of DPA on learning and morale.
- Model daily activity in classes where teachers are supportive.
- Use success stories from participating classes to support your proposals.
- To make scheduling seem less complicated, suggest taking a few minutes off each class and developing a schoolwide schedule. Add activities only on days that the children do not already have physical education.
- Make the program as convenient as possible for the teachers. Start small and encourage often.
- Listen to feedback, and involve those with concerns in finding solutions.
- Always reflect, assess, and revise the program to meet changing needs.
- Regularly communicate to parents the positive aspects of DPA in the school newsletter. Emphasize that academics are being enhanced, not compromised.
- To sustain the program, provide administrative teams with ideas and reminders for DPA at staff meetings, profile your program in the local media, and celebrate the small achievements.
- Use any space that is available to you—in addition to classrooms and the gymnasium, use playing fields, playgrounds, asphalt open areas, hallways, lunchrooms, and multipurpose areas.
- Apply for grants to help pay for music and equipment. Approach the school district or school council to see if funds are available for DPA.

CELEBRATING SUCCESS

Celebrate from the start of the first DPA meeting to the end of the school year. Thank leaders and all those involved for coming to training sessions, and congratulate their display of commitment. Celebrate participants' and leaders' enthusiasm throughout the program and at the end of the year so the whole school and community can be proud of the program (appendix C contains inspiring success stories from four schools). You can also celebrate staff, student, and leader participation and enthusiasm through newsletter articles, PA announcements (e.g., class, leader, and teacher of the week), and community newspaper recognition.

PROVIDING INCENTIVES

You may increase support from all stakeholders with incentive programs. To sustain your program will require reflection, assessment, and revision of the program to meet changing needs on an ongoing basis. Fortunately there are many resources available to help when revision is needed.

The following two areas provide additional incentives within your program: activity bag and extra gymnasium time.

Activity Bag

- The activity bag can be filled with any of the following items: Hacky Sacks, footballs, soccer balls, basketballs, tennis balls, scoops, and skipping ropes. Include any items that will keep your participants busy during recess or break times.

- A great way to get children and youth active is to reward them with equipment. A bag of equipment can be awarded as a draw prize (e.g., to a class who all walked to school on a Walking Wednesday). Every week you can have a new winner.

- An activity bag can also be rotated to all the classrooms. The activities can be included in a surprise package with the necessary equipment, or the bag can include equipment that can be used on the playground.

- Your school could have a Stop, Drop, and Exercise session when the activity bag comes to your classroom. You can see how many classes have participated by the end of the day.

- Pass the Bass is another fun option. A basket gets passed along to the classrooms. The basket includes a rubber fish, an activity card, any necessary equipment, and a camera. When the bass gets to the classroom, the class participates in the designated activity and takes pictures of the participants before passing the bass to the next class.

Extra Gymnasium Time

- Running out of money for prizes? Reward your students with extra free gymnasium time or use of the gymnasium at recess, lunch, or after school.

- The winners of this extra gymnasium time could be determined with a draw or based on greatest participation during recess. The winners could gain the use of the gymnasium for their favorite activities. Allow them to invite 10 to 20 of their friends to participate with them.

SUMMARY

All DPA programs depend on support from administrators, teachers, students, parents, and communities to be successful. To encourage support, the DPA goals must be communicated and progress noted. Securing financial support will continue to be a challenge, but we have presented several ideas to help you. Finally, be sure to celebrate the success of your program and provide rewards to the students.

CHAPTER 11

Assessing Your DPA Program

Assessment and evaluation of a daily physical activity program are important aspects of determining the program's success. When using any method of implementing a DPA program, baseline assessment and ongoing assessment are needed for feedback and improvement. The most important indicator of success is an increase in activity levels of both students and staff. Assessment and evaluation of a program should include schoolwide (administration), teacher, parent, and student perspectives.

When assessing a DPA program, it is important not only to observe participation levels but also to discuss activities and program implementation with both students and other staff. During the evaluation, strengths of the program as well as challenges or areas of improvement are identified. Student and staff participation, enjoyment, and effort are key factors to consider for DPA. DPA programs can be measured schoolwide by administrators, teachers, peers of students, and student self-assessment.

SCHOOLWIDE ASSESSMENT

Alberta Education (2006) provides the following questions to guide DPA program assessment and improvement:

- Has there been an increase in student physical activity levels?
- Did the DPA plan provide for activities that ensure all students have the opportunity to achieve a measure of success?
- Was there an increase in student knowledge of the benefits of physical activity to an active, healthy lifestyle?
- Was there an increase in understanding of the intended expectations of DPA by students, staff, and parents or guardians?
- Did DPA-related professional development increase staff confidence and comfort levels with the delivery of DPA?
- Were improvements made to the physical environment of the school (e.g., bulletin board displays, optimized use of activity space)?
- Were there opportunities for staff sharing of "craft knowledge" or best practices?

- Did the DPA plan support staff responsibility?
- Were there new opportunities for staff to critically assess past practices, eliminate barriers, and risk trying new strategies and activities?
- Has there been ongoing and regularly scheduled DPA monitoring and assessment?

A second way for school administrators to assess how they are doing is by evaluating the following indicators of DPA:

- school plan
- leadership and organization
- scheduling, facilitation, and delivery
- use of resources and equipment
- evaluation of fitness goals

Table 11.1 is a sample rubric that can be used for schoolwide assessment. For this example, 20 minutes is used as the objective. Schools may also use this rubric to determine in which areas the school should work toward improving.

TEACHER ASSESSMENT

Teachers contribute to the assessment of DPA by reflecting on their own practice and through observation or use of a rubric of student participation and effort. To identify professional practice strengths and challenges of DPA, teachers can complete a simple analysis or reflection (see table 11.2).

Teachers can assess students' involvement in DPA using indicators such as participation, effort, and safety (see table 11.3).

PEER ASSESSMENT

Peer assessment involves students discussing the activity and their effort with a friend or classmate. Peer discussion with a "health buddy" enhances the learning experience for both participants. Have participants discuss their activity. They can ask each other questions such as "Did it get your heart beating fast?" "Did you like it?" "Would you do it again on your own, outside of class?" "What else could you do at home to get your heart beating fast?"

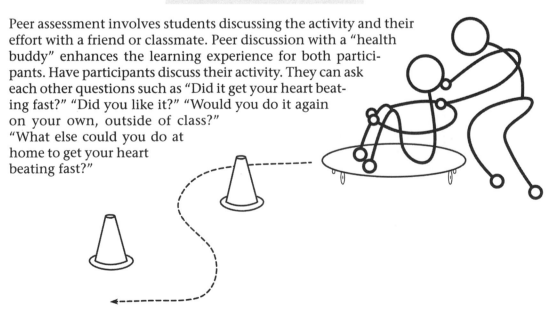

Table 11.1 Halton District School Board DPA Implementation Rubric

QDF criteria	Stage 1 Preimplementation	Stage 2 Implementation	Stage 3 Building capacity	Stage 4 Sustaining capacity
School plan	School's DPA plan of action begins to focus on leadership, organization, communication, scheduling, and resources. It has been shared with staff and they have been asked for input.	DPA plan of action focuses on leadership, organization, communication, scheduling, and resources. It is beginning to address the specific needs of the school facility, staff, and students. It is beginning to encourage all staff and students to buy in and make it happen.	DPA plan of action for entire year builds in accountability for inclusion into program with feedback from staff and students and addresses the specific needs of the school facility, staff, and students. Administrators, teachers, and students see the link between daily physical activity and learning. DPA is emerging as part of school culture.	DPA plan of action incorporates a DPA model specific to the needs of the facility, staff, and students that allows for flexibility and adaptability. Staff meeting and PD agendas are used to maintain the focus. Administrators, teachers, and students see the link between daily physical activity and learning. DPA is part of the school culture.
Leadership and organization	A DPA key teacher has been identified and administration is aware of DPA. DPA sessions are led mostly by the same person. DPA activities are limited in variety (e.g., students follow an exercise routine). Students are not involved in leadership roles.	A DPA key teacher has attended some in-service opportunities. A DPA organizing committee and administrative leadership for DPA exist. DPA sessions are led mostly by the same person and provide some variety. Students occasionally lead activities.	A DPA key teacher and a committee attend workshops or in-services and involve others. Administrative support and leadership for DPA exist. DPA sessions are led by a few individuals and a variety of DPA activities are offered (e.g., stations, classroom activities, mass activities, celebration events). Students are trained as leaders of DPA activities.	A DPA key teacher and committee attend workshops or in-services and involve and mentor others. Administrative support, leadership, and active participation in DPA exist. DPA sessions are led by a variety of people (e.g., teachers, students) and a variety of DPA activities are offered using a variety of resources (e.g., DVDs, station instructions). Students develop and lead DPA activities.

(continued)

Table 11.1 Halton District School Board DPA Implementation Rubric *(continued)*

QDF criteria	Stage 1 Preimplementation	Stage 2 Implementation	Stage 3 Building capacity	Stage 4 Sustaining capacity
Scheduling, facilities, and delivery	A minimum of 10 minutes of physical activity may take place in PE classes. No formal scheduling of classes for DPA on non-PE days. Safety is addressed in DPA activities.	A minimum of 10 minutes of physical activity takes place in PE classes only. An individual teacher schedules several classes for DPA sessions on non-PE days. Safety is addressed in DPA activities.	A minimum of 20 minutes of physical activity takes place in PE classes, and a committee schedules DPA activities for all classes on non-PE days. Safety is addressed in DPA activities.	A minimum of 20 minutes of physical activity takes place in PE classes. All teachers schedule DPA daily. DPA occurs every day in whatever location is appropriate for the classroom plan of the day. Safety is addressed in DPA activities.
Resources and equipment	DPA kit resources are used on a limited basis. Staff has access to equipment and resources.	DPA kit resources and Ophea cards are used in the delivery of the program. Staff and students have access to equipment and resources.	All of the resource materials are used and additional materials are developed by the DPA team. A process is in place for easy access to equipment and resources by all staff and students. Equipment and resources are repaired or replaced as needed.	All of the resource material is used and additional materials are developed by the DPA team and student leaders. A process is in place for easy access to equipment and resources by all staff and students. Equipment and resources are repaired or replaced as needed, and new, innovative items are purchased.
Evaluation	Students begin to set own fitness goals in order to lead a healthy, active lifestyle. Staff tracks student involvement.	Students sometimes set their own goals and sometimes monitor their own progress in leading a healthy, active lifestyle. Staff tracks student involvement and the progress of the DPA initiative.	Students set their own goals and monitor their personal progress in leading a healthy, active lifestyle. Tools are used to assess student participation in DPA, and data are sometimes used as part of the reporting process.	Students set their personal goals, monitor their personal progress, and track their success in leading a healthy, active lifestyle. Tools are developed to assess student participation in DPA, and data are used as part of the reporting process.

Reprinted, by permission, from S. Amos, D. Caourville, and D. Hastings, 2006, *Quality daily fitness: Making it happen in Halton* (Burlington, ON: Halton District Schools), 204.

Table 11.2 How Are We Doing?

What's going well already at my school?	What can I do to increase daily physical activity at my school?
☐	☐
☐	☐
☐	☐
☐	☐
☐	☐
☐	☐
☐	☐
☐	☐
☐	☐
☐	☐
☐	☐
☐	☐
☐	☐

Table 11.3 Participation Rubric

Indicators	Level 1	Level 2	Level 3	Level 4
Participation Participates in DPA	Participates actively only with constant encouragement	Participates actively, needing only occasional encouragement	Requires no encouragement to participate actively	Participates actively in a manner that encourages others to participate
Effort Sustains participation at a moderate to vigorous level for a minimum of 20 minutes (i.e., constantly moving, elevated heart rate, monitoring heart rate or pulse, perspiring, breathing harder, talk test)	Infrequently works hard (i.e., goes through the motions)	Sometimes works hard with encouragement	Regularly demonstrates a determined effort	Almost always strives for personal best

(continued)

Table 11.3 Participation Rubric   (continued)

Indicators	Level 1	Level 2	Level 3	Level 4
Safety procedures Dresses appropriately to participate (i.e., suitable footwear, no hanging jewelry) Uses equipment and facility in an appropriate manner while participating	Requires constant reminders regarding dressing appropriately to participate Requires constant reminders regarding the use of equipment and facility in an appropriate manner while participating	Requires occasional reminders regarding dressing appropriately to participate in physical activity Requires occasional reminders regarding the use of equipment and facility in an appropriate manner while participating	Regularly dresses appropriately to safely participate in physical activity Follows safety procedures when using equipment and facilities while participating	Almost always dresses appropriately to safely participate in physical activity Follows safety procedures when using equipment and facilities while participating, and encourages others to do so

Reprinted, by permission, from S. Amos, D. Caourville, and D. Hastings, 2006, *Quality daily fitness: Making it happen in Halton* (Burlington, ON: Halton District Schools), 204; Ontario HPE Curriculum Support, Appendix G, Ophea.

STUDENT SELF-ASSESSMENT

Self-assessment helps students understand their own bodies and how physical activity feels to them. For elementary-level students, it is important to discuss what participation in physical activity would feel and look like. By introducing students to simple tests, they can gauge their level of participation.

- Breath sound check: Ask students to observe the sounds of their breathing and the difference in sounds at various intensities of activity. They should exert themselves so that they clearly hear themselves breathing hard.
- Talk test: Assesses students' level of exertion. If they can carry on a simple conversation while exercising, they are moving at a good pace.
- Heart rate check: Students in grade four or older should know how to find their pulse and measure it. Older students can be taught to calculate a rough estimate of their target heart rate to assess their participation. To calculate target heart rate, subtract your age from 220 and then find 70 to 85 percent of the difference to get your target heart rate in beats per minute. Divide by six to get the required number of heartbeats in 10 seconds.

The teacher can ask students to self-assess, which also provides feedback to the teacher. Here are two ways:

- Four-finger flash: Ask students to give themselves a rating for participation by holding up fingers, 4 being the highest and 1 being the lowest. Select one or two students to explain why they gave themselves the rating they did by providing an explanation with examples.
- Thumbs up or down: Thumbs up indicates full participation; thumbs down indicates poor participation. Ask students to show you with their thumbs up, down, or somewhere in between the amount of effort they believed they exhibited while participating. Ask students to explain their assessment.

SUMMARY

Implementation of a daily physical activity program requires monitoring and assessment to ensure its success. It is important that teachers, administrators, students, parents, and guardians understand how physical activity can help them achieve a healthy lifestyle. This resource provides easy-to-use advice, ideas, and solutions to help schools incorporate daily physical activity into the lives of all students. Classroom teachers need not become physical education specialists, but they will learn how to emphasize the fun and enjoyment of physical activity. The ideas presented here can be used by all classroom teachers to engage children in daily physical activity. Our goal is to encourage and provide opportunities for children to make active living and learning a way of life. Everybody move!

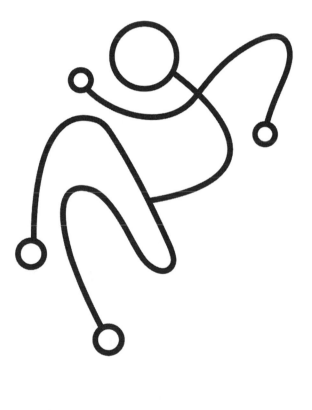

Glossary of Fitness Activities

bench dips—Start by sitting on a bench with legs out straight and hands beside hips, holding on to edge of bench. Lower hips to floor, then extend arms to bring hips up again. (This works the triceps muscles at the back of the arms.) Alternatively, participant can be in crab-walk position and lower arms down and up again.

bent-knee curl-ups (crunches)—While lying on back, place feet on the floor and keep knees bent. With arms at sides or crossed on chest, slowly raise torso so that abdominals contract. Slowly bring back down to floor and repeat. Ensure that lower back remains in contact with floor at all times.

bicycle pumps—Lie on back and lift buttocks and hips off the floor into the air (push feet to ceiling, and pedal feet as if riding a bike). Can be done on a desk or any other surface where your feet can come off the ground and pretend to pedal.

bicycle sit-ups—Lie on back with hands by temples. Touch right elbow to left knee, then left elbow to right knee and repeat.

calf lifts—While standing, rise slowly onto both feet so you are on your toes. Feel the calf muscles tighten. Slowly go back down, and repeat in a controlled manner.

crab walk—Start by sitting on the floor with knees bent, feet on floor. Lean back on hands and raise buttocks off the floor. Walk on hands and feet.

crunches—see bent-knee curl-ups.

dips—See bench dips.

Energizer Bunny hops—Jump on two feet in a random but energetic pattern, pumping your arms as you jump.

gluteal kicks—Jog on the spot, with heels kicking your buttocks.

lunges—These can be done to the side or front. Start standing with feet together. To lunge forward, step forward on right leg, making sure that knee flexes over top of foot (not beyond). Keep back straight. Push off of right foot to return to standing position. Repeat on left leg. Side lunge is a step to the right, flexing right knee while keeping left leg straight. Push off of right leg to return to standing position. Repeat on left side.

mountain climber—Starting in a push-up position on the floor, alternately bring knees up to chest.

Nordic skiing—Slide right foot back while left arm swings straight forward. Return to center, then repeat with left foot and right arm.

push-ups (modified)—Keep torso straight just like a full push-up, but rest on knees rather than feet. The only movement comes from bending the arms.

tuck jumps—Jump high in the air while bringing both knees toward your abdomen. Land softly on both feet.

up and down—Reach both arms overhead, then crouch down to touch the floor.

V sit—Sit on the floor, leaning back slightly keeping your lower back off the floor. Lift both legs up so your body is in a V position.

zigzag jumps—With feet together, jump diagonally to right and then left forward or backward.

Sample Newsletter

Promoting your program creates awareness of it, informs people about it, and elicits a response from students whom you most want to involve, staff whom you will need support from, and parents whom you want to inspire to continue your good work in the home. Creating informative and attractive newsletters is a great way to promote your daily physical activity program.

In terms of the students, you want to create an awareness of the exciting opportunities available to student leaders, inform them about how to get involved, and elicit an excitement about becoming a student leader. Pictures of other student leaders enjoying their experiences, and parts of engaging stories of the benefits of student leaders, are great ways to grab students' attention.

Staff love to get involved in successful programs. A polished newsletter that demonstrates the benefits of the program and shows other colleagues having fun and furthering educational goals through the integration of daily physical activity is an important tool in advancing the cause and engaging further staff support and involvement.

Parents love to see their children engaged in positive and healthy activities. Parent councils may be quicker to share some occasional financial resources when they see teachers putting in extra time for the overall health of the student body.

Your program is a good one. Be sure to make people more aware of it, inform them about how to get involved, and engage them through an effective newsletter. The newsletter on the next few pages demonstrates one way to effectively promote your good work.

Daily Physical Activity

Why is Daily Physical Activity (DPA) important?

- Improves overall health and quality of life
- Provides opportunities for social interaction, and improves social and moral development
- Reduces risk of developing adult diseases (cardiovascular disease, type 2 diabetes, some cancers, obesity, osteoporosis and symptoms of arthritis)
- Gives a sense of well-being and improves self-esteem
- Reduces anxiety and stress
- Contributes to a positive school culture, decreases vandalism, and is a positive intervention strategy for behavior management
- Improves cognitive functioning and academic achievement in school

This year marks the beginning of daily physical activity in all schools in our state. The Department of Education has declared that every child in our state will receive 30 minutes of daily physical activity that increases heart rate and develops muscular strength, flexibility, and endurance.

We are committed to your child here at school. Ask your child how DPA went today! Take interest in what your child is doing to stay active and healthy, both physically and mentally!

A little exercise is good, but more is better. Please make an extra effort to use active transportation, such as walking or cycling, to get to school every day this week.

Daily Physical Activity Super Week

From September 15 to 19 we will be celebrating daily physical activity through assemblies and discussions focused on making active choices. Here is a list of our special activities:

Moving Monday: We will kick off the week with everybody funky moving on the blacktop. Join us from 9:00 a.m. to 9:30 a.m.

Tag Tuesday: Join us on the field for a giant tag event. Grades 1 and 2 begin at 9:00 a.m., grades 3 to 5 at 9:30 a.m., and grades 6 to 8 at 10:00 a.m. You're "it"!

Workout Wednesday: DPA student leaders will be leading an aerobics session in the back playground from 9:00 a.m. to 9:30 a.m. Come and join in as you drop your children off. Toddlers to granddads are welcome!

Jumpin' Thumpin' Thursday: We will be holding a jump rope event at lunchtime. Please encourage your children to bring a skipping rope if they have one. If they don't, it will be a good excuse to buy one.

Fitness Friday: We will be walking or running around the perimeter of the school grounds from 10 a.m. to 10:30 a.m. Everyone is welcome to join us! ⊚

Dressed for Success

For safety reasons, proper running shoes are required for participating in our activities every day. Please provide your child with shoes that are supportive and have nonmarking soles. Elevated running shoes are not permitted.

Comfortable loose-fitting clothes allow for ease of movement and increase enjoyment of physical activity.

If you have any questions regarding footwear or suitable clothing, please feel free to contact Mrs. Ima Runner at the school. ⊚

DPA Student Leaders

As part of student leadership and ongoing commitment to daily physical activity, many of our grade 7 and 8 students will be trained to deliver simple games, activities, and moves to music for our younger school population through DPA. Our goal is to provide our leaders with the skills necessary in order to be positive role models for the younger students by setting a great example of participating in daily physical activity. We welcome parents and community members to join our student leader training team. For more information, contact Mr. B. Active at the school.

Each month in our DPA newsletter, we will feature an outstanding leader who demonstrates enthusiasm and commitment to the delivery of the DPA program at school. Their initiative, dedication, and efforts are appreciated, and we want them to be recognized. High five! ⊚

Success Stories

F our success stories are included in the following pages and provide inspiration for your program. Take a look through these stories to gain ideas and motivation to carry out your program.

ROBERT LITTLE PUBLIC SCHOOL

Robert Little Public School in Acton, Ontario, is the star of the Halton District School Board. It is a small school of approximately 400 students, from JK to grade 5, whose commitment to DPA (daily physical activity) has established it as a leader in advocating for children's quality daily fitness. Robert Little is proud to have received the national PHE Canada (Physical Health and Education Canada) award for the school's quality physical education and CIRA Ontario's Outstanding Intramural Achievement Award six years in a row for promoting fun, active participation for all. The Halton District School Board was a pioneer in DPA and refers to it as QDF (quality daily fitness). Robert Little has experienced successful programs because of the support of administration and staff. Having everybody moving toward the shared goal of children's physical health is a key component.

At Robert Little, grade 4 and 5 students are invited to sign up to be DPA/QDF leaders in September. These students make a yearlong commitment to train as fitness leaders and role models for other students as they lead activities and routines in classrooms and the gym. The leaders are taught activities and moving-to-music routines from *Everybody Move!* At a specified time each day, a leader will announce on the PA system, "Two minutes to QDF." With this cue, leaders proceed in pairs to their designated classrooms to lead the DPA activities and routines. With the next PA message ("It's time for Active School Challenge! Let's get active, Robert Little! Active bodies equal active minds!"), music is played over the PA system to classrooms that do not have physical activity that day, and everybody is active. Often the whole school participates at the same time in DPA.

Robert Little provides many opportunities for students and staff to be physically active through participation in the following activities and events during the school year: International Walk to School Day/Week, Guinness World Records World Record Walk, Walking Wednesdays, I Walk Club, Terry Fox Run, Go Active! Fitness Challenge, grade 4 and 5 ski and snowboard trips, Living Outside the Box TV Turnoff Week activities and Family Fun Night, Robert Little Community Walkabout, dance-a-thons, play days, Fit Week events, and national CAHPERD challenges. Students can also participate in cross country running, track and field, basketball, and volleyball.

All Robert Little students and staff are actively involved in regular celebrations and assemblies when Active Assembly music (*Everybody Move!* songs where students perform the corresponding upper-body movements while sitting) is played as the students enter and exit the gym and as energizers during long assemblies.

Another popular activity at Robert Little is the Junior Everybody Dance Club (grades 3 to 5). Students in this club learn easy dances in a positive, nonthreatening environment and perform regularly at assemblies, concerts, and community events and even at the Mississauga Living Arts Centre in Toronto. The Mini Everybody Dance Club (grade 2) learns basic dance steps and routines and enjoys performing on stage also.

To get everybody moving, a DPA program must have enthusiastic leaders and staff and motivating music, and it must be *fun*! Remember . . . active bodies equal active minds.

C.H. NORTON PUBLIC SCHOOL

C.H. Norton Public School in Burlington, Ontario, has been committed to DPA for the past six years with the belief that students need to develop physical literacy as well as the ABCs and 123s of learning. The school, which is home to more than 670 JK-8 students, has received many awards in recognition for its outstanding contributions to keeping students active in their day-to-day experiences at school, including PHE Canada's distinguished gold and platinum levels, Ophea's Super Active School recognition, and CIRA Ontario's Outstanding Intramural Achievement Award. In addition to an outstanding physical education program in which all students participate a minimum of twice per week, all students receive 20 minutes of daily physical activity on days throughout the year when they do not have physical education class. As well, students have the opportunity to participate in a wide variety of intramurals that are designed to engage all children in fun, active sessions that continue to promote the merits of a healthy, active lifestyle.

The success of the program over the years lies mainly in the dedication and commitment of the staff, and in particular, the staff that make up the DPA committee. This energetic group of people meet, plan, and deliver a variety of school challenges throughout the year that are enjoyed by all the members of the school community. As the school year begins each September, the focus is on walking—walking across Canada from the east to the west coast; walking back from the west to the east coast; or following Terry Fox's route and completing his Marathon of Hope. The students and staff get motivated to "step it up" and rack up as many steps as possible as they track their progress on a large wall-sized map. Daily results are tracked and recorded on the map. Each time a new milestone is reached, students read Canadian trivia, facts, or historic information over the PA system pertaining to the city that has been reached. As progress is made traveling the country, the whole school celebrates the achievements of a community effort because it takes everybody working as a team to achieve the end result.

During the first month of September, students in grades 7 and 8 are busy preparing for the yearlong job of being DPA leaders. These dedicated students train to learn activities and dances that can be done for 20 minutes in a primary or junior classroom where they can lead by example. The leaders leave their own physical education warm-up portion of class and spend this time leading other students in DPA routines and games that are designed to increase heart rates and get kids moving as part of the daily physical activity mandated by the Ministry of Education. Once their DPA session is completed in the primary and junior classrooms, leaders return to class and rejoin their peers for the lesson. The benefits of this type of delivery of the DPA program are huge—leadership opportunities for intermediate students; quality activities for primary and junior students; virtually no stress on the teacher present to deliver a program; and a win–win situation for all!

C.H. Norton has also participated in many whole-school events, some of which are national challenges. It is not unusual to see posters or hear announcements that advertise and promote the next school challenge. Events include Walk to School, SpecTAGular, Toonie for Terry fund-raiser for cancer research, dance-a-thons, moooove-a-thons, play days, intramurals, Winter Active and Summer Active challenges, TV Turnoff, Hoops for Heart, and Jump Rope for Heart. The school has been recognized nationally for its top fund-raising efforts for the Heart and Stroke Foundation of Ontario. Furthermore, the students also have many opportunities to involve themselves in active living options such as skipping teams, fitness and aerobics clubs, hip-hop dance clubs, cross country, volleyball, basketball, track and field, and soccer intramural and interschool sporting activities.

Students at C.H. Norton recognize the importance of physical activity and value the opportunities they have to be active as well as the rewards of their efforts. DPA is a scheduled event in all classrooms, and this has become part of living healthy, active lives. Teachers understand that the physical breaks provide a much needed breather during classroom work periods, and students experience a greatly improved time on task after the fitness breaks. The school runs on a "balanced day" schedule, which means that all students learn in blocks of time. The balanced day has also provided the school with more flexibility to run intramural programs during one or both of the scheduled breaks in the day. This allows students an opportunity to get active in the gym with a variety of programs. To provide for an optimal learning environment, all students receive a nutritious snack every Tuesday and Thursday. Teams of parent volunteers run the snack program, and they are responsible for buying and preparing the food, organizing the snack trays for each classroom every week, and doing the required clean-up.

With the commitment of our administration, parents, teachers, support staff, and students, C.H. Norton Public School has become a leader in physical literacy and is recognized for its outstanding efforts to continue to improve the fitness levels of our students. In this day and age when the obesity levels of our children are hitting unprecedented highs, the school community works collectively as a team to combat this increasing problem. The school believes in the saying that "every journey begins with one step," and the steps have been adding up as milestones are reached in the ever-evolving physical challenges that are provided for the students. We anticipate that these small steps will translate into a future filled with a multitude of healthy, active living opportunities for most, if not all, of our school community.

HIGHLAND PUBLIC SCHOOL

We at Highland Public School in Cambridge, Ontario, have made a commitment to promote healthy, active lifestyles for children on a daily basis. Three years ago, we began a program of daily physical activity (DPA) where the entire school body is exercising for at least 20 minutes each day all at the same time.

At the beginning of the year, I hold a meeting for any junior students who are interested in becoming a DPA leader. These students make a yearlong commitment to this initiative and are outstanding role models for the younger students. I begin by teaching them three different routines to music; a warm-up song, a cardio component, and a cool-down song. Once they are confident enough, they then go in pairs into all of the classes within the school to lead the other students through the moves as the music is being played over the PA system. If you were to walk through the school during this time, you would see the students eagerly participating and many of them singing along. It really is an amazing sight to see! They are having so much fun that I don't think they even realize they are exercising anymore. As a result of this program, I truly believe that Highland students have developed not only a greater appreciation of the importance of staying healthy and active but also a love for music and dance!

There are many opportunities throughout the year for the DPA leaders to celebrate and share their talents. We end each of our monthly assemblies with DPA. This means that all DPA leaders come up to the front of the gym and lead more than

500 students and teachers through the routines together. When you have everyone singing, smiling, and moving at the same time, it is so easy to see why this program is such a success and beneficial to all. The leaders have also had the opportunity to travel to different elementary schools within our community to demonstrate a variety of the routines. This allows me the opportunity to share with other teachers how the program works at Highland and answer any questions they might have.

The feedback we have received from the parent community is amazing. They love the program and support it in any way they can. Because their children were constantly talking about daily physical activity at home, many of them began coming into the school to see the kids in action. I then began hearing things like, "I can barely get my child out the door because she is so busy dancing and singing her way through her regular morning routine! I love it!" or "What a great way to model the importance of staying active, even in the classrooms," and "They are even teaching us the routines at home!" I can say with confidence, that this is a very contagious program that is being shared at school level, in the home, and within our community.

MORTON WAY PUBLIC SCHOOL

If you want to motivate students to move, play music. Then teach them some routines to music. There are many terrific routines described in this resource, and it is simple to make up your own to your favorite tunes, using the Funky Moves cards found in chapter 7. At Morton Way Public School in Brampton, Ontario, performing routines to music has become, well, routine. The students in grades 1 to 5 are exposed to dozens of dances in physical education and music classes, in daily physical activity, as warm-ups for cross country running, during assemblies, and even out on the playground when the stereo is rolled outside for Fitness Fridays.

Every year, Morton Way holds a Moo-vathon (with a cow theme and plenty of incentives to get students "moo-ving"). Students collect money from sponsors, then, on Moo-vathon day, they come to the gym by grade level for 40 minutes of nonstop routines, most of which are featured in *Everybody Move!*

On inclement weather days when the students can't go outside for recess, either all the primary students or all the junior students are invited to the gym to get active to music. This gives the students another opportunity to get their hearts pounding and their muscles moving. At the end of the recess, students are ready to get back to learning in the classroom.

Active Assemblies are also part of the Morton Way culture. As students enter and exit the gym, familiar music is played. As soon as students hear the music, they start moving, even if they are still in the halls. The Active Assemblies routines feature hand movements, so they can be performed while seated. Entries and exits run smoothly, as students are engaged in the activity, and everyone is left with smiles on their faces. The Active Assemblies routines are included in this resource. They include Agadoo, Bring It All Back, Get Ready for This, Hey Baby, Lollipop, and Reach.

Music seems to put everyone in a good mood, and it does wonders for school spirit. Give it a try—it's contagious!

References
and Resources

Activ8kids! New York State School Nutrition and Physical Activity Best Practices Toolkit. www.health .state.ny.us/prevention/obesity/activ8kids.

Alberta Education. 2005. Daily physical activity school handbook.www.education.alberta.ca/ teachers/program/pe/resources/dpahandbook.aspx.

Alberta Education. 2006. *Daily physical activity: A handbook for grades 1-9 schools.* Edmonton, AB: Alberta Education.

Alberta Education. 2008. Daily physical activity survey report: Executive summary. http:// education.alberta.ca/media/756345/dpaexesum.pdf.

Alsager, D. 1977. *Intramural programming in Ohio high schools.* Unpublished manuscript, Miami University, Oxford, Ohio: Author. http://iweb.aahperd.org/naspe/template .cfm?template=ns_children.html.

Barthel, S., and D. Gleddie. 2005. *Run, jump, and throw: Implementing daily physical activity in Alberta schools.*

Booth, M., A.D. Okely, E. Denney-Wilson, L. Hardy, B. Yang, and T. Dobbins. 2006. *NSW schools physical activity and nutrition survey (SPANS) 2004: Full report.* New South Wales Department of Health, Centre for Epidemiology and Research. Available: www.health.nsw .gov.au/pubs/2006/spans/index.html.

British Columbia Ministry of Education. 2009. Daily physical activity: Tracking tools. www .bced.gov.bc.ca/dpa/log.htm.

Byl, J. 2002. *Intramural recreation.* Champaign, IL: Human Kinetics.

CAHPERD. 2006a. DPA in your class. *Clipboard for Physical Education and Intramural,* 8 (2).

CAHPERD. 2006b. Two breaks a day for PDA. *Fit to Learn* (Fall).

Canadian Fitness and Lifestyle Research Institute 1995. Physical activity monitor. Available: www.cflri.ca/eng/provincial_data/pam1995/index.php.

Canadian Fitness and Lifestyle Research Institute 2002. Physical activity monitor. Available: www.cflri.ca/eng/statistics/surveys/pam2002.php.

Centers for Disease Control and Prevention. 1997. Guidelines for school and community programs to promote lifelong physical activity among young people. MMWR 1997;46 (no. RR-6): inclusive page numbers. Available: ftp://ftp.cdc.gov/pub/publications/mmwr/ rr/rr4606.pdf.

Centers for Disease Control and Prevention. 2004. Participation in high school physical education: United States, 1991-2003. *Morbidity and Mortality Weekly Report* 53 (36): 844-847.

Delaware Department of Education. 2007. Brader 4th graders demonstrate Fitnessgram. www .doe.state.de.us/news/2007/0504.shtml.

Drowatzky, K., and J. Drowatzky. 2000. Physical activity and bone mineral density. *Clinical Kinesiology* 54 (2): 28-35.

Ethnier, J.L., P.M. Nowell, D.M. Landers, and B.A. Shibley. 2006. A meta-regression to examine the relationship between aerobic fitness and cognitive performance. *Brain Research Reviews* 52: 119-130.

Fishburne, G. J., and D.A. Harper-Tarr. 1992. An analysis of the typical elementary school timetable: A concern for health and fitness. In T. Williams, L. Almond, and A. Sparkes (Eds). *Sport and Physical Activity: Moving Toward Excellence,* pp. 362-375. London: E & FN Spon.

Freedman, D. S., W.H. Dietz, S.R. Srinivasn, and G.S. Berenson. 1999. The relation of over-weight to cardiovascular risk factors among children and adolescents: The Bogalusa Heart Study. *Pediatrics, 103*(6 Pt 1): 1175-1182.

Freedman, D.S., L.K. Khan, W.H. Dietz, S.R. Srinivason, and G.S. Berenson. 2001. Relationship of childhood obesity to coronary heart disease risk factors in adulthood: The Bogalusa heart study. *Pediatrics* 108 (3): 712-718.

Froelicher, V., and E. Froelicher. 1991. Cardiovascular benefits of physical activity. In *Benefits of leisure*, edited by B.L. Driver, P.J. Brown, and G.L. Pederson, 59-72. State College, PA: Venture Publishing.

Getting Fit Texas! 2008. www.dshs.state.tx.us/obesity/pdf/PromotorasFlyer.pdf.

Government of Alberta. 2009. Daily physical activity initiative. Available: http://education .alberta.ca/teachers/resources/dpa.aspx.

Grunbaum, J.A., L. Kann, S. Kinchen, J. Ross, J. Hawkins, R. Lowry, W.A. Harris, T. McMarus, D. Chyen, and J. Collins. 2004. Youth risk behavior surveillance: United States, 2003. *Morbidity and Mortality Weekly Report* 53 (SS-2): 1-95.

Howe, C.A., and P. Freedson. 2008. Physical activity and academic performance. PCPFS E-newsletter (Fall). www.fitness.gov/enewsletter/fall2008/featurearticle.html.

Hunter, G., M. Gamman, and D. Hester. 2000. Obesity-prone children can benefit from high-intensity exercise. *Strength and Conditioning Journal* 22 (1): 51-54.

Keays, J.J., and K.R. Allison. 1995. The effects of regular moderate to vigorous physical activity on student outcomes: A review. *Canadian Journal of Public Health* 86 (1): 62-65.

McKay, S.L., I.S. Reid, M.S. Tremblay, and R. Pelletier. 1996. *The impact of recreation on youth in transition to adulthood: A focus on youth at risk.* In *Youth in transition: Perspectives on research and policy*, edited by B. Galway and J. Hudson, pp. 284-292. Toronto: Thompson.

National Association for Sport and Physical Education. 2004. *Physical activity for children: A statement of guidelines for children ages 5-12.* Reston, VA: Author.

National Association for Sport and Physical Education. 2006. *Shape of the nation report.* www .aahperd.org/Naspe/ShapeOfTheNation.

National Association for Sport and Physical Education. 2008. *Comprehensive school physical activity programs.* [Position statement]. Reston, VA: Author. http://iweb.aahperd.org/naspe/ pdf_files/CSPAP_Online.pdf.

New Hampshire Department of Education. 2009. NH Schools must recommend daily physical activity. www.Ed.State.nh.us/education/news/physical_activity.htm.

Norrie, Hon. M., and Mustard, J. F. 1999. Early years study: Final report. The Canadian Institute for Advanced Research.

Ontario Education. 2006. Healthy schools: Daily physical activity in schools. Guide for school boards. www.edu.gov.on.ca/eng/teachers/dpa_boards.pdf.

Paffenbarger, R., R. Hyde, and A. Dow. 1991. Health benefits of physical activity. In *Benefits of leisure*, edited by B.L. Driver, P.J. Brown, and G.L. Pederson, 49-57. State College, PA: Venture Publishing.

Queensland Government. 2008. Smart moves: Physical activity programs in Queensland State Schools. http://education.qld.gov.au/schools/healthy/docs/smart-moves-web.pdf.

Queensland Government. 2009. Daily physical activity guide for schools. www.sportrec.qld .gov.au/Publications/DailyPhysicalActivityGuideforSchools.aspx.

Schools Come Alive. 2005. Daily physical activity/education for the elementary generalist teacher: Participant handout. www.schoolscomealive.org/files /__DPA%20Elem%20Generalist%20with%20Inclusion.pdf.

Shields, D.L.L, and B.J.L. Bredemeier. 1994. *Character development and physical activity.* Champaign, IL: Human Kinetics.

Shields, M. 2006. Overweight Canadian children and adolescents. Nutrition: Findings of the Canadian Community Health Survey, (Ottawa: Statistics Canada) 82-620-MWE.

Statistics Canada. 2001. *National longitudinal survey of children and youth: Participation in activities.* Ottawa: Statistics Canada. www.statcan.gc.ca/pub/82-620-m/2005001/pdf/4193660-eng.pdf.

Statistics Canada 2003. Canadian Community Health Survey (CCHS) – Cycle 1.1 [online]. Available: www.statcan.ca/english/concepts/health/index.htm.

Texas Department of State Health Services. 2008. *Promotoras in action.* www.dshs.state.tx.us/obesity/physicalactivitypromot.shtm.

The President's Council on Physical Fitness and Sports Research Digest. 1997. Youth sport in America: An overview. In Corbin, C. & B. Pangrazi. (Eds.). *Research Digest, 2* (11).

Tomporowski, P.D., C.L. Davies, P.H. Millar, and J.A. Naglieri. 2007. Exercise and children's intelligence, cognition, and academic performance. *Educational Psychology Review* 20, 111-131.

Tudor-Locke, C., R. Bell, and A. Myers. 2000. Revisiting the role of physical activity and exercise in the treatment of type 2 diabetes. *Canadian Journal of Applied Physiology 25* (6): 466-491.

U.S. Department of Health and Human Services. 1996. *Physical activity and health: A report of the Surgeon General.* Atlanta, GA: Centers for Disease Control and Prevention (CDC), National Center for Chronic Disease Prevention and Health Promotion. Available: www.cdc.gov/nccdphp/sgr/sgr.htm.

U.S. Department of Health and Human Services. 2008a. HHS announces physical activity guidelines for Americans. www.hhs.gov/news/press/2008pres/10/20081007a.html.

U.S. Department of Health and Human Services. 2008b. Progress review: Physical activity and fitness. www.healthypeople.gov/data/2010prog/focus22.

U.S. Department of Health and Human Services. 2009. Physical activity facts. www.fitness.gov/resources_factsheet.htm.

About CIRA Ontario

CIRA Ontario is a nonprofit organization that encourages, promotes, and develops active living, healthy lifestyles, and personal growth through various programs in educational and recreational settings. The organization began as the Ontario Intramural Recreation Association in 1969 and became the Canadian Intramural Recreation Association of Ontario. The first edition of *Everybody Move!* was produced in 2005 and translated into French in 2007. The organization has had numerous other resources published to promote healthy and active living.

About the Contributors

John Byl, PhD, is the president of CIRA Ontario and a professor of physical education at Redeemer University College in Ancaster, Ontario. Dr. Byl has contributed chapters to 15 books. He authored several books, including *Intramural Recreation* and *Organizing Successful Tournaments*, and has coauthored several books, including *Chicken and Noodle Games* and *Christian Paths to Health and Wellness*. He is the winner of several professional awards and is a regular workshop leader. Dr. Byl has a special interest in promoting fun, active participation for all children (especially his five grandchildren) and developing and maintaining personal wellness.

Marie Burland has combined her backgrounds in fitness, marketing, and education in creating the Everybody Move! initiatives to promote enhanced physical activity in the primary grades.

Since 2001, Marie has taught junior kindergarten to grade 4 at Robert Little Public School in Acton, Ontario. Her areas of focus are physical and health education, dance and drama, and music. Marie believes that active bodies equal active minds. She started a quality daily fitness program at Robert Little by training students in grades 4 and 5 to be fitness leaders. She also initiated the Everybody Dance Club for students in grades 2 to 5 at the school; the club has over 50 members who perform at assemblies and local venues.

Marie has received several leadership and recognition awards from CIRA Ontario, the Halton District School Board, and the Town of Halton Hills. She has been instrumental in earning the Provincial CIRA Ontario Outstanding Intramural Achievement Awards and the National Physical and Health Education Canada Awards every year for her school by providing students with quality physical education and promoting healthy, active children.

Mary Dyck teaches sport psychology, sport sociology, motor learning, and sport management at the University of Lethbridge in Alberta, Canada. Previously, Mary taught at Redeemer University College in Ontario and Trinity Western University in British Columbia. She is a certified level III coach in volleyball and soccer. She currently uses her talents and training to coach youth soccer and high school volleyball. Mary began coaching in 1980 and has coached youth programs, college soccer teams, university soccer and volleyball teams, and provincial soccer teams at the under-13, under-16, and under-18 levels. Mary is also a coaching course conductor for the Alberta Soccer Association and Alberta Volleyball Association, which allows her to meet and mentor new coaches. Mary's research agenda involves online citizenship and cyberbullying, encouraging and managing daily physical activity programs in schools, social and moral development of teens through physical education, and empowering girls in sport and physical activity. For fun, Mary plays on several soccer teams and pulls weeds in her garden to relieve stress.

Michelle Hearn began her teaching career with the Halton District School Board in 1998. During her seven years at George Kennedy Public School, she coached volleyball and track and field, and she assisted in organizing and implementing a quality daily fitness program at both the school and regional level. In 2005, Michelle was presented with an Award of Distinction for her role as a cowriter of the *Everybody Move!* resource. Since then she has had the opportunity to continue working with CIRA to in-service other school boards across the province.

When Michelle began teaching with the Waterloo District School Board, she continued to coach a variety of sports teams and also brought her dance and fitness background to Highland Public School. Once again, she quickly implemented a QDF program where junior students were offered a leadership opportunity within the school. During the next few years, Michelle worked with her superintendent and a few other colleagues to develop a series of workshops that provided training for two representatives from each of the 100 elementary schools in the region. Michelle is a certified fitness instructor and a voleyball player; she's currently enjoying her time off with her baby boy.

Kirstin Schwass has been a teacher since 1992; she has worked as an elementary physical education teacher since 1999. In 2002, Kirstin received Peel's Award of Excellence for outstanding contributions to public education. Kirstin holds a BPE and an MA in psychology of sport. Kirstin's passion is helping children lead active, healthy lives at school and in their community. She is the coordinator of Morton Way Public School's Walk and Roll program, which encourages active ways of getting to and from school in an effort to attain cleaner air, safer streets, and healthy bodies. This program won the International Walk to School Award in 2005. Kirstin was recognized as a Hometown Hero by the City of Brampton with the 2008 Children's Safety Award. Kirstin serves on the Peel District School Board's Daily Physical Activity Implementation Committee, the Health and Physical Education Conference Committee, and School Communities Action Project. She is also an executive member of CIRA Ontario. Kirstin contributed to the writing of several CIRA Ontario resources and is a regular presenter at workshops. Every weekend in the winter, Kirstin can be found on the ski slopes coaching her ski racing team of 8- to 10-year-old athletes. She has been involved in dryland and snow training since 1981. In 2003, Kirstin and her 13-year-old son trained to run the 21.5 kilometers to her school on International Walk to School Day. Since then, Kirstin has been a long-distance runner and has completed five half marathons with her son and four full marathons, including the Boston Marathon, with her husband. Kirstin is an avid canoeist and enjoys wilderness canoe tripping with her husband and three children.

Milena "Mel" Trojanovic has been an elementary school teacher specializing in health and physical education with the Halton District School Board since 1991. While teaching at C.H. Norton Public School in Burlington, Ontario, she has reached many students through wellness and believes in physical literacy for all her students. Under her guidance, the school has received many recognition awards, including the Ontario Physical and Health Education Association's distinction as a Super Active School, the CIRA Ontario Outstanding

Intramural Achievement Award, Physical and Health Education Canada's Platinum standing for providing excellence in daily physical activity promotion, and recognition from the Heart and Stroke Foundation for fund-raising efforts for Jump Rope for Heart. She is a regular workshop presenter for both CIRA Ontario projects as well as board initiatives throughout the year and loves the opportunity to share her knowledge with others. She has two children who enjoy many activities, including basketball, hockey, football, and dance. She also has one very supportive husband!

DVD-ROM
User Instructions

SYSTEM REQUIREMENTS

You can use this DVD-ROM on either a Windows-based PC or a Macintosh computer.

Windows

- IBM PC compatible with Pentium processor
- Windows 98/2000/XP/Vista
- Adobe Reader 8.0
- 4x DVD-ROM drive

Macintosh

- Power Mac recommended
- System 10.4 or higher
- Adobe Reader
- 4x DVD-ROM drive

USER INSTRUCTIONS

The PDFs on this DVD-ROM can be accessed only with a DVD-ROM drive in a computer (not a DVD player on a television). To access the PDFs, follow these instructions:

Windows

1. Place DVD-ROM in the DVD-ROM drive of your computer.
2. Double-click on the My Computer icon from your desktop.
3. Right-click on the DVD-ROM drive.

Macintosh

1. Place DVD-ROM in the DVD-ROM drive of your computer.
2. Double-click the DVD icon on your desktop.
3. Double-click on the Documents and Resources folder.
4. Select the PDF file that you want to view or print.

Note: You must have Adobe Acrobat Reader to view the PDF files.

For customer support, contact technical support:
Phone: 217-351-5076 Monday through Friday (excluding holidays) between 7:00 a.m. and 7:00 p.m. (CST).
Fax: 217-351-2674
E-mail: support@hkusa.com

CD CONTENTS

Dances Demonstrated on DVD

1. Smile (2:38)
2. Eddie the Razor (2:30)
3. Motion Motion (3:11)
4. Marching Circus (2:01)
5. Gringo (3:02)
6. Latinique (3:36)
7. Dream Machine (2:56)
8. Ethno Tension (1:51)
9. Aerobics (5:03)
10. Boxercise (9:50)

Latin Mix

11. Mambo Jumbo (2:45)
12. Cumbia Urbana (3:30)
13. Reggaeton (2:06)
14. Lucky 6 (2:07)

Get-Moving Songs

15. Rock From 9, Jive till 5 (1:50)
16. Rock Shot (3:33)
17. Rock and Roll (2:25)
18. Bjorn Again (1:35)
19. Naughty Noises (2:21)
20. Mission Improbable (2:19)
21. Stadium Rock (3:41)

Elementary Circuit

22. Madison Scat (0:35)
23. Benny and the Gladiators (0:35)
24. Mozerella (0:35)
25. Speedy Mosquito (0:35)
26. Crazy Farm (0:35)
27. Chicken Ribs (0:35)
28. Groovy Toons (0:36)

High School Circuit

29. Bad Johnny (0:35)
30. Beach Beat (0:37)
31. Halfpipe (0:35)
32. Street Runner (0:36)
33. Standup (0:35)
34. Feel Good Factor (0:34)
35. Champions (0:36)

Cool-Down Songs

36. Jammin' Mon (2:03)
37. Shammusa (3:38)

DVD CONTENTS

Eddie the Razor (2:29)
Motion Motion (3:10)
Marching Circus (2:01)
Gringo (3:00)
Latinique (3:36)
Dream Machine (2:56)
Ethno Tension (1:50)
Aerobics (4:58)
Boxercise (9:47)

Latin Mix: Mambo Jumbo (2:44)
Latin Mix: Cumbia Urbana (3:29)
Latin Mix: Reggaeton (2:02)
Latin Mix: Lucky 6 (2:05)
Smile (2:37)
Smile Yoga (2:37)
Funky Move Demonstrations
Reproducible Activity Cards